BELIEVING, KNOWING, CONVINCED

DAVE THOMAS

Copyright © 2011 Coltshill Publishing
95 Castle Road, Mumbles, Swansea SA3 5TA.
davidthomas11350@hotmail.com

BELIEVING, KNOWING, CONVINCED
ISBN 978-1-4709-8581-3

Printed and distributed by lulu.com

Further copies of this book can be obtained
via lulu.com; amazon.com; retail outlets.

Other books by author
Justice - ISBN 0-9545733-0-7 (First edition © 2003)
Justice - ISBN 978-1-4466-3717-3 (Second edition © 2010)
Life-Giving Spirit - ISBN 978-1-4466-8635-5

No part of this publication may be reproduced or transmitted
in any form or by any means, electronic or mechanical,
including photocopy, recording or any information
storage and retrieval system, without permission
in writing from the publisher.

Scripture quotations taken from The Holy Bible,
New International Version © 1973, 1978, 1984, 2011
by International Bible Society, unless otherwise stated.

Used by permission of Hodder & Stoughton Ltd.
All rights reserved.

Cover design by Coastline Graphic Design
graham.champion@gmail.com

CONTENTS

BELIEVING

1. Forgiven – A New Creation	1 – 4
2. Forgiven – The Curse Removed	5 – 8
3. Forgiven – Made Holy	9 – 12
4. Forgiven – Reconciled to God	13 – 16
5. Forgiven – The New Self	17 – 20
6. Forgiven – The Fruit of Change	21 – 24
7. Forgiven – No Condemnation	25 – 28
8. Forgiving Others	29 – 32
9. Belonging	33 – 36
10. Seed	37 – 40
11. Seed Faith – Roots	41 – 44
12. Seed Faith – Reproducing	45 – 48
13. Seed Faith – Sowing & Reaping	49 – 52
14. Seed Faith – Enduring	53 – 56
15. The Kingdom of God – His Nature	57 – 60
16. The Kingdom of God – A New Beginning	61 – 64
17. The Kingdom of God – A New Life	65 – 68
18. Prayer – Seeking God's Kingdom	69 – 72
19. Prayer – Listening	73 – 76
20. Prayer – Watch and Pray	77 – 80

KNOWING

21. Know Him Better	81 – 84
22. Knowing Ourselves Better	85 – 88
23. Moments	89 – 92
24. Hearing His Voice – A Listening Ear	93 – 96
25. Hearing His Voice – Obedience	97 – 100
26. Inheritance	101 – 104
27. Renewing our Mind – Transformed	105 – 108
28. Renewing our Mind – Persevering	109 – 112
29. Renewing our Mind – Set Free	113 – 116

Contd.

CONTENTS

KNOWING contd

30. The Anointing	117 – 120
31. Fulfilling Scripture – Authority	121 – 124
32. Fulfilling Scripture – Spirit and Life	125 – 128
33. Fulfilling Scripture – Resting	129 – 132
34. Grace and Works	133 – 136
35. The Trial of our Faith	137 – 140
36. Character	141 – 144
37. Standing	145 – 148
38. No Turning Back	149 – 152
39. Freedom	153 – 156
40. Freedom to Expand	157 – 160

CONVINCED

41. Convinced	161 – 164
42. Firmly Established	165 – 168
43. Confidence	169 – 172
44. Assurance	173 – 176
45. Benediction	177 – 180
Summary	181

LIST OF ABREVIATIONS

OLD TESTAMENT

Genesis	Gen
Exodus	Ex
Deuteronomy	Deut
Samuel	Sam
Proverbs	Prov
Jeremiah	Jer
Habakkuk	Hab

NEW TESTAMENT

Matthew	Matt
Romans	Rom
Corinthians	Cor
Galatians	Gal
Ephesians	Eph
Philippians	Phil
Colossians	Col
Thessalonians	Thess
Timothy	Tim
Hebrews	Heb
Revelation	Rev

ACKNOWLEDGEMENT

Much appreciation to
John Spiller, Jackie Davies, Rev. Charles Durke,
for their editing and advice.

I would also like to thank Raymonde Harries
for his design of the front cover,
and Graham Champion for his technical expertise
in the production of the cover, and book.

ABOUT THE AUTHOR

He is a retired Police Officer, who lives with his wife, Irene, in Swansea, South Wales. They have three children.

For the past thirty years he has formed and led home-groups.

INTRODUCTION

I know whom I have believed, and am convinced that He is able to guard what I have entrusted to Him for that day (2 Timothy 1:12).

In the above verse, Paul explained that there is a process that we go through as a Christian in order to mature in our faith; we first of all **believe**; we get to **know**, and then become **convinced**. This principle applies to our general faith; but it also affects each of the individual truths within the Word of God.

For example, Christians *believe* the Word of God when it states that there is *no condemnation for those who are in Christ Jesus* (Romans 8:1). But when we fall short in some area of our life, do we find it difficult to live in the fullness of that Scripture? The reason this occurs is usually because we have not *held onto the Word* (John 8:31); we have let it slip from our grasp. We have not persevered, and as a consequence of this we do not *know it with certainty* (John 17:8; Luke 1:4). We have not become *convinced* of its truth.

Jesus had many followers, but not everyone continued with Him, or learned to apply His words to their lives. It is the *holding onto His Word* that makes us a true disciple.

If you hold to my teaching, you are really my disciples. *Then you will know the truth, and the truth will set you free* (John 8:31).

John 6:30-69 records the occasion when Jesus sought to take His followers further on in their revelation of Him – *I am the bread of life* (John 6:35). When He challenged them to get a deeper understanding of what it means to be in relationship with Him, many of His disciples said, *"This is a hard teaching. Who can accept it?"* (John 6:60). Sadly, many turned back.

contd.

INTRODUCTION contd

Jesus asked those who remained if they were still committed. Peter answered on their behalf:

*"Lord, to whom shall we go? You have the words of eternal life. **We believe and know** that you are the Holy One of God"* (John 6:68-69).

Those disciples had gone from **believing to knowing**.

Jesus later said of them – ***they know with certainty*** (John 17:8); they were *convinced*. The same principle applies to us.

The timescale of this process depends upon how long it takes for us to *accept His words* (John 17:8), and live by them. We learn to truly hold onto His Word.

Jesus said, "The words I have spoken to you are spirit and they are life" (John 6:63).

CHAPTER ONE

FORGIVEN – A NEW CREATION

God did not send His Son into the world to condemn the world*, but to save the world through Him* (John 3:17).

When we are born again we enter a 'state of forgiveness.' It is not a place that we enter just at certain times. It is a permanent residence. It is not based upon the level of goodness within us. It is purely the result of what Jesus did for us at the Cross, when He took upon Himself all the sin of the world.

God reconciled the world to Himself through Christ, not counting men's sins against them*...God made Christ who had no sin to be sin for us, so that **in Christ we might become the righteousness of God*** (2 Corinthians 5:19-21).

Righteousness means – 'right-standing' with God. This is not obtained by trying harder, self-improvement, or through any attempted righteousness on our own part. We receive the righteousness of God within us when we accept Christ Jesus into our lives – *This righteousness from God comes through faith in Jesus Christ to all who believe* (Rom. 3:22).

Your spirit is alive because of (Christ's) righteousness (Romans 8:10).

Christians are in that 'state of forgiveness' because – *God reconciled the world to Himself through Christ, not counting men's sins against them* (2 Cor. 5:19). Formerly, sin caused a barrier between us and God. The Lord Jesus brought about reconciliation. It is not temporary, or based upon our performance. It is permanent because of Christ's presence within us, by the Holy Spirit. For us to lose that 'state of forgiveness' it would necessitate the Lord leaving us. But He has promised – *Never will I leave you; never will I forsake you* (Heb. 13:5).

CHRIST'S RIGHTEOUSNESS

*You were dead in your transgressions and sins...gratifying the cravings of **our sinful nature**...we were by nature objects of wrath...But God, who is rich in mercy, **made us alive with Christ** even when we were dead in transgressions – it is by grace you have been saved* (Ephesians 2:1-5).

The part of us that is *made alive with Christ* is our spirit. This is clearly shown in Romans 8:10 – *If Christ is in you, your body is dead because of sin, yet **your spirit is alive because of (Christ's) righteousness**.*

Adam, like us, comprised of – *spirit, soul and body* (1 Thess. 5:23). Up until that point in time when Adam sinned his spirit was perfect. He was not created with a sin nature. It was only after he sinned that his spirit changed, and sin entered the world. As a result of that change, every person since Adam is now born with a spirit that has a sin nature.

***Sin entered the world through one man**, and death through sin, and in this way death came to all men, because all sinned* (Romans 5:12).

Adam's disobedience brought sin and death into the world, but Jesus' obedience brought life.

*For if, by the trespass of one man (Adam), death reigned through that one man, how much more will those who **receive God's abundant provision of grace and of the gift of righteousness** reign in life through the one man, Jesus Christ* (Romans 5:17).

We *receive the gift of (Christ's) righteousness* when He enters our life when we **believe**; we are born again. We receive a new nature in our spirit, namely that of God's divine nature.

SIN NATURE REMOVED

Therefore, if anyone is in Christ, he is a new creation; **the old has gone, the new has come!** (2 Corinthians 5:17).

What is the *old* that has gone, and what is the *new* that has come when we are *in Christ*? What change takes place within us when we enter that 'state of forgiveness?'

In Christ you were also circumcised, in the putting off of the sinful nature, *not with a circumcision done by the hands of men but with the circumcision done by Christ* (Colossians 2:11).

*His divine power has given us everything we need for life and Godliness...***so that you may participate in the divine nature*** (2 Peter 1:3-4).

In the Old Testament, circumcision was an outward sign of covenant relationship with God. What was cut off was not kept. It was no longer a part of the person. It was discarded. It was something that was of the past. Similarly, when Christ, by the Holy Spirit enters our spirit, He cuts off the sin nature, and replaces it with the divine nature. The *circumcision*, which He completes upon us, removes the old. It is discarded. We become a *new creation* because of His divine nature coming into us.

When you were dead in your sins and in the uncircumcision of your sinful nature, God made you alive with Christ. *He forgave us all our sins* (Colossians 2:13).

When our old sin nature is removed, and in its place we receive of the divine nature, it is not a gradual process; it is a complete cutting away. This new birth, becoming a *new creation*, takes place in our spirit, when the Lord Jesus enters our life – *The (Holy) Spirit gives birth to (our) spirit* (John 3:6).

THE DIVINE NATURE RECEIVED

Since the creation of the world, God's invisible qualities – **His eternal power and divine nature** *– have been clearly seen* (Romans 1:20).

God's divine nature is revealed in one statement – *God is love* (1 John 4:8). Everything about Him flows from this truth. Some of His characteristics that are expressed from His love are that He is compassionate (Psalm 145:8); faithful (Psalm 33:4); good (Psalm 34:8); gracious (Ephesians 1:6); Holy (Exodus 15:11); just (Isaiah 61:8); merciful (1 Peter 1:3); patient (2 Peter 3:9); righteous (Psalm 89:14); unchangeable (Matthew 24:35); truthful (John 17:17).

Everything about His nature is revealed to us in His Word. If we want to know God, we look at Jesus – *The Word became flesh and made His dwelling among us* (John 1:14).

Scripture says of Jesus that He is – *full of grace and truth* (John 1:14). When we are born again we are – *given fullness in Christ* (Col. 2:10). We are literally – *given everything we need for life and Godliness* (2 Peter 1:3).

Therefore, every born-again believer has the capacity, because of having received of the fullness of the divine nature within us, to respond to others in the same manner as Jesus, who is – *full of grace and truth* (John 1:14).

Through the Lord Jesus, the divine nature is in our spirit where He dwells by the Holy Spirit. It is fair to say that we do not always respond to others as Jesus does. But, by meditating upon His Word and being led by His Spirit, our soul realm will be changed. Our mind, heart and emotions will be transformed, to become more like Him – **Being transformed into His (Christ's) likeness with ever-increasing glory** (2 Cor. 3:18).

CHAPTER TWO

FORGIVEN – THE CURSE REMOVED

*For if, by the trespass of the one man (Adam), death reigned through that one man, how much more will those who receive God's abundant provision of grace and of **the gift of righteousness** reign in life through the one man, Jesus Christ* (Romans 5:17).

We are born again by the grace of God (His unmerited favour) through faith – *By grace you have been saved, through faith* (Eph. 2:8). Through those acts of grace and faith we receive *the gift of righteousness* (right-standing with God).

Abraham received righteousness by faith – *Abraham believed the Lord, and He credited it to Abraham as righteousness* (Gen. 15:6; Rom. 4:3).

The moment that we **believe** by placing faith in the Lord Jesus, His death and resurrection, we receive His salvation; and are accepted as righteous before our Heavenly Father.

*The words "It was credited to him (Abraham)" were written not for him alone, but also for us, to whom **God will credit righteousness – for us who believe in Him** who raised Jesus our Lord from the dead* (Romans 4:23-24).

The righteousness that we receive is nothing that we can take credit for. It is not by any of our works, or because of any goodness on our part. We are accepted by God in His own righteousness that He **imputes** into us because of faith in Christ.

As a result of receiving His righteousness we can always come before our Father. Sin, although serious, no longer disqualifies us from His presence, disinherits us from salvation, or removes us from our position in Christ Jesus.

THE LAW

I would not have known what sin was except through the Law (Romans 7:7).

The Law of the Old Testament consisted of the Ten Commandments, together with other instructions. It was helpful, in that it enabled us to know the difference between right and wrong. But it was never meant to be the means by which we have a relationship with our Father. Abraham was accepted by God because of his faith, before the Law was given (Gen. 15:6).

The Law came because of mans' continued lawlessness. In the giving of the Law, God's love and mercy is revealed; He did not want mankind to destroy itself. A set of Godly principles were given for man to live by.

The Law reveals what we instinctively know, but try to ignore; that even with God's Law we fall short. The Law proved once and for all that we need a Saviour.

The Law was put in charge to lead us to Christ *that we might be justified by faith. Now that faith has come,* ***we are no longer under the supervision of the Law*** (Galatians 3:24-25).

The purpose of the Law, therefore, was not just for us to obey a set of rules. It was given to show us our inability to be righteous in our own standing. We needed a Saviour, who was without sin, so that we could have right-standing before God in our Saviour's righteousness.

But now a righteousness from God, apart from law, has been made known*, to which the Law and the Prophets testify.* ***This righteousness from God comes through faith in Jesus Christ*** *to all who believe* (Romans 3:21).

GOD'S WRATH

*Since we have now been justified by His (Jesus') blood, how much more shall we be **saved from God's wrath through Him*** (Romans 5:9).

When someone sinned under the Old Covenant they were disobeying a set of rules under the Law. In order for their sin to be 'covered over' a sacrifice was offered, which had to be without defect. Jesus is – *The lamb without blemish or defect* (1 Peter 1:19), who does not simply cover over our sin; He totally removes the need for any further sacrifice for our individual sins.

*Christ entered the Most Holy Place **once for all** by His own blood, having **obtained eternal redemption*** (Hebrews 9:12).

Our eternal redemption was established by Jesus' death and resurrection. He cancelled the Old Covenant, establishing a new one – *a superior covenant, founded on better promises* (Heb. 8:6). At the same time that Jesus was being physically nailed to the Cross, God was *cancelling the written code with its regulations*, which identified our guilt, *nailing it to the Cross*.

*God forgave us all our sins, **having cancelled the written code, with its regulations**, that was against us and that stood opposed to us; **He took it away, nailing it to the Cross*** (Colossians 2:13-14).

Because of Jesus, a Christian does not experience God's wrath – ***God did not appoint us to suffer wrath** but to receive salvation through our Lord Jesus Christ* (1 Thess. 5:9).

God's wrath will only be displayed towards those who do not accept Jesus as their Saviour – *Whoever believes in the Son has eternal life, but whoever rejects the Son will not see life, for God's wrath remains on him* (John 3:36).

BLESSED AND NOT CURSED

***Christ redeemed us from the curse of the Law** by becoming a curse for us* (Galatians 3:13).

The Old Testament Law consisted of the moral (ethical behaviour); civil (legal system); ceremonial (sacrifices, festivals, priestly activities). Blessings or curses depended upon obedience

***All these blessings** will come upon you and accompany you if you obey the Lord your God...* (Deuteronomy 28:1-14). *However, if you do not obey the Lord your God and do not carefully follow all His commands and decrees, **all these curses** will come upon you* (Deuteronomy 28:15-68).

All the blessings involved increase; whereas the curses included defeat, sickness, poverty and fear, because they incurred the wrath of God. However, Jesus took upon Himself all of God's wrath. He paid the penalty with His own blood, shed on the Cross – ***becoming a curse for us*** (Gal. 3:13).

There are consequences to our actions. Born-again believers can bring all manner of bad things upon themselves through committing sin. But the consequences are not because of God's wrath. This has been removed from a Christian.

Jesus came to *fulfil the Law and the prophets.* Nothing would *disappear from the law until everything was accomplished* (Matt. 5:17). He was the perfect sacrifice the Law required; it was *accomplished.* He also fulfilled all prophecies.

Everything was *accomplished.* The Lord declared at the Cross – ***"It is finished"*** (John 19:30). He had told His disciples that in order to enter Heaven, their righteousness had to *surpass that of the Pharisees* (Matt. 5:20). Christ's own righteousness accomplishes this, which He imputes into us (2 Cor. 5:21).

CHAPTER THREE

FORGIVEN – MADE HOLY

But now a righteousness from God, apart from Law, has been made known, to which the Law and the prophets testify. ***This righteousness from God comes through faith in Jesus Christ to all who believe*** (Romans 3:21-22).

When we repent of our sin, and ask Christ Jesus to be our Saviour, our sins are completely forgiven. This does not apply only until the next time that we sin. It means that a born-again believer's past, present, and even future sins are forgiven.

This occurs because of what Jesus accomplished at the Cross when He offered His blood as an offering for the sins of the world – *Christ entered the Most Holy Place once for all by His own blood, having obtained* **eternal redemption** (Heb. 9:12).

He (Christ Jesus) is able to save completely those who come to God through Him, because He always lives to intercede for them (Hebrews 7:25).

Any sin that we commit after we are saved is not held against us, because the Lord Jesus' own righteousness has been **imputed** into us; we are *saved completely*. When the Father looks at us, He sees Christ within us – *If Christ is in you…your spirit is alive because of (His) righteousness* (Rom. 8:10).

God made Him (Jesus) who had no sin to be sin for us, so that **in Him we might become the righteousness of God** (2 Corinthians 5:21).

There is a consequence to sin as we shall examine in Chapter Six. But sin itself does not alter our 'righteous standing' before God. This is because of Christ's righteousness within us. The only way that can be affected would be if He were to leave us.

HOLINESS

***We have been made holy** through the sacrifice of the body of Jesus Christ once for all...By one sacrifice **He (Christ Jesus) has made perfect for ever** those who are being made holy* (Hebrews 10:10; 14).

When Christ Jesus comes into our life by His Spirit at our salvation we enter a 'state of forgiveness, righteousness and holiness.' The reason this happens is solely because of the Lord's presence within us. We enter that 'state' by *God's grace through faith*; not by us trying to become holy by our works.

By grace you have been saved, through faith *– and this not from yourselves, it is the gift of God – not by works, so that no-one can boast* (Ephesians 2:8).

Hebrews 10:10 states that a Christian – *has been made holy.* This happens through Christ's presence entering our spirit, thereby making it – *alive because of (His) righteousness* (Rom. 8:10) – *we participate in the divine nature* (2 Peter 1:4).

*He has brought us into the Kingdom of the Son he loves, in whom **we have redemption, the forgiveness of sins*** (Colossians 1:13-14).

After we are born again, we *train ourselves to be Godly* (1 Tim. 4:7); *Be holy in all you do* (1 Peter 1:15). We do so, not in order to be accepted by the Lord. We live like this in response to having already been accepted by Him. We are able to live in such a manner because – *His divine power has given us everything we need for life and Godliness* (2 Peter 1:3).

We are not trying to attain holiness. We live an increasingly holy life in response to a 'state of holiness' that we receive because of Christ's divine nature coming into us.

SEALED

*Having believed, you were **marked in Him with a seal**, the promised Holy Spirit* (Ephesians 1:13).

When we are born again, and enter into relationship with the Lord, we are *marked in Him with a seal*. The word *seal* (sphragizo) indicates – **'ownership, security and destination.'** It is not something that is gained over time. It has the meaning of definiteness and completeness; a finished act.

We are not in an on-off relationship with the Lord dependent upon our performance, or if we sin. We are in a 'state of forgiveness, righteousness and holiness' because we have placed our faith in the Lord Jesus, who has enabled us to be completely forgiven through His shed blood on the Cross. It is a finished act – *We have been made holy through…Jesus Christ* (Heb. 10:10).

***You were redeemed**…with the precious blood of Christ, a lamb without blemish or defect* (1 Peter 1:18-19).

When the Lord Jesus enters our spirit, by the Holy Spirit, He places a *seal* over our spirit. The devil has no access to our spirit because it is sealed. The only way that the devil can influence us is through our soul and body. Our spirit is completely cleansed of any sin because it is filled and sealed by the Holy Spirit. His presence within us does not come and go.

When we sin, after being saved, it is not because of us still having a sin nature; that has been *circumcised*, cut off by Christ at our salvation (Col. 2:11). Sin occurs because our mind, heart, will and emotions are in the process of being *transformed* (Rom. 12:2) into His image. Our spirit is instantly changed; but the transformation of our human nature in our soul, to become more like the divine nature within our spirit, occurs over time. We change by applying His Word, and being led by the Holy Spirit.

OWNERSHIP, SECURITY, DESTINATION

*God anointed us, **set His seal of ownership on us**, and put His Spirit in our hearts as a deposit, guaranteeing what is to come* (2 Corinthians 1:21-22).

OWNERSHIP – When we ask Christ Jesus to be our Saviour and Lord we willingly relinquish ownership of our life. We acknowledge that we are no longer the 'god' of our life; He is God. When He takes ownership it is for now, and into eternity. He places His Spirit within us as a *guarantee*. This is not the sort of guarantee that the world gives, which is for a limited period, and full of conditions. His love is unconditional, and is eternal.

The Lord does not abandon ownership of us if we do not achieve a certain standard, or if we sin and make mistakes. He has made us a promise – *Never will I leave you; never will I forsake you* (Heb. 13:5); **His seal of ownership is on us**.

SECURITY – The Lord has told us that we are completely secure in Him – ***No-one can snatch them out of my hand*** (John 10:28). There are situations in life which can cause us to feel vulnerable, whether it is through affliction by the devil, or through committing sin and having doubt. At those times we have a choice to make. Do we give in to feelings, and falsely believe that the Lord has left us; or do we stand upon what the Word of God clearly states – *He will never forsake us*.

DESTINATION – The destiny of a born-again believer is assured. In fact, Scripture states that our destiny has already been accomplished in part - **God raised us up with Christ** *and seated us with Him in the Heavenly realms in Christ* (Eph. 2:6).

Jesus said, "In my Father's house are many rooms; if it were not so, I would have told you. ***I am going there to prepare a place for you****"* (John 14:2).

CHAPTER FOUR

FORGIVEN – RECONCILED TO GOD

Jesus said, "It is finished." *With that, He bowed His head and gave up His spirit* (John 19:30).

At the beginning of His ministry, Jesus said – *"I have come to **fulfil** the Law and the prophets"* (Matt. 5:17). He is *the Lamb of God, who takes away the sin of the world* (John 1:29). He is the only one who **fulfilled** the perfect requirements of the Law. The night before His trial, He declared to the Father – *I have brought you glory on earth by **completing the work** you gave me to do* (John 17:4). At the Cross He declared – *It is finished*.

Everything that Jesus came to do was finished. There was nothing left undone. He fulfilled everything, and in so doing brought about reconciliation between God and man by His sacrificial death on the Cross.

When Jesus was crucified, the curtain in the Temple that separated the Holy Place from the Most Holy Place was torn in two (Luke 23:45). Formerly, only the High Priest had been allowed to enter past the curtain. Because the Lord offered His own blood for the sins of the entire world, man can now enter the Most Holy Place straight into God's presence in Jesus' name.

The *finished* work of the Lord Jesus also enabled God to enter man, whereby we are born again by the Holy Spirit. When Christ comes into our life by the Spirit we are *saved completely* (Heb. 7:25). Being born again is a finished act.

The *finished* work of salvation means that we are justified, reconciled, redeemed, adopted, sanctified and glorified. These are finished acts in our spirit. Sanctification and glorification are also a continuing process in our soul, in the same way that we are righteous in Christ and respond to Him by living righteously.

JUSTIFIED & RECONCILED

A man is not justified by observing the Law, but by faith in Jesus Christ (Galatians 2:16).

Justified is a legal term meaning acquittal from guilt. It pronounces us as being just. It basically means – as if we had never sinned – *Since **we have been justified through faith**, we have peace with God through our Lord Jesus Christ* (Rom 5:1). This means that there is a specific time when we are *justified*.

This occurs when we enter into relationship with God through faith in Christ – ***By grace you have been saved through faith**...not by works* (Eph. 2:8-9). This means that neither before, nor after salvation, can we rely on our own works to be *justified*.

The world is **reconciled** to God through Jesus' sacrificial death on the Cross. Formerly, sin caused a barrier between us and God. We required a means by which we could come into, and remain, in relationship/friendship with God. We needed to be *reconciled* to Him – *God demonstrates His own love for us in this: while we were still sinners, Christ died for us* (Rom. 5:8).

***God reconciled the world to Himself in Christ**, not counting men's sins against them* (2 Corinthians 5:19).

Sin has now been dealt with for the entire world. People do not go to Hell because of the individual sins they commit. They go there because of the one sin of rejecting Christ Jesus as their Saviour, who paid the penalty for sin by His sacrificial death – *Whoever believes in the Son has eternal life, but **whoever rejects the Son will not see life, for God's wrath remains on Him*** (John 3:36). When we **believe**, God's wrath is removed.

As a result of our sins no longer being held against us, a born-again believer is both *justified* and *reconciled* to God.

REDEEMED & ADOPTED

What the Law was powerless to do…God did by sending His own son…to be a sin offering (Romans 8:3).

Redeemed (Gal. 3:13) has the meaning of 'buying out,' as in the case of purchasing a slave with a view of setting him free – *It is for freedom that Christ has set us free* (Gal. 5:1). Being *justified* means that we are acquitted; our sins are no longer held against us. *Redemption* reveals that through Christ we are set free. There is no penalty for our sin that we have to pay.

Deuteronomy chapter 28 records the blessings and curses of keeping the Law, which was a list of commandments that the Israelite nation had to keep. Failure to do so was a sin, for which a sacrifice was made to cover the sin. When Jesus was crucified, He took on Himself the penalty for sin that we should have borne – **Christ redeemed us from the curse of the Law by becoming a curse for us** (Gal. 3:13).

Adopted – In explaining adoption, Paul referred to a custom in Roman times, when the eldest son, usually around the age of fourteen, was considered ready to become the heir to his father. He was already a son, but it was not until he was 'adopted' that he was recognised as an heir to his father's inheritance.

Every person is a child of God (Acts 17:28-29). However, it is only when we are born again through Christ Jesus that we are adopted into God's family, and become sons and heirs of Him – *Since you are a son, God had made you also an heir* (Gal. 4:7).

In adoption today, the child is not the same biologically. But the adoption by our Heavenly Father means that when the Holy Spirit enters our life, He *begets* us (John 3:3-7) – *To all who received Christ…He gave the right to become children of God…born not of human decision, but **born of God*** (John 1:12).

SANCTIFIED & GLORIFIED

To those sanctified in Christ Jesus and called to be holy (1 Corinthians 1:2).

Sanctified means 'set apart to God,' and living a holy life in a manner that is in accordance with that purpose. It has a similar meaning to consecration, as used in the Old Testament.

When we are born again we enter a 'state of sanctification.' We are declared *sanctified in Christ Jesus* (1 Cor. 1:2). We are set apart to God through our Lord Jesus. Our life changes because we are no longer the 'god' of our lives; He is God. There is a change of ownership.

From that point in time, and for the rest of our earthly lives, there follows a process of sanctification in our lives through the application of the Word of God, and the guidance of the Spirit.

When we become a Christian we are **glorified** in Christ Jesus. The Holy Spirit *gives birth to our spirit* (John 3:6); the presence of the Lord enters our life. In so doing, His glory is manifested in us. A fundamental change occurs.

Those God called, He also justified; **those He justified, He also glorified** (Romans 8:30).

And we, who with unveiled faces all reflect the Lord's glory, are being **transformed into His likeness with ever-increasing glory***, which comes from the Lord, who is the Spirit* (2 Corinthians 3:18).

The above verse states *ever-increasing glory*. In order for it to *increase* in us it has to be in existence within us, namely our spirit. Our response to Him is to be *transformed* (Rom. 12:2) in our mind and heart, so that our soul also reveals His glory.

CHAPTER FIVE

FORGIVEN – THE NEW SELF

Blessed is the man whose sin the Lord will never count against him (Romans 4:8; Psalm 32:1-2).

When we understand that, once we are born again, we are in a 'state' of forgiveness, righteousness and holiness, two questions obviously arise – Firstly, does it matter if we sin because we are already forgiven? Secondly, is there a need to confess and repent of sin? The Apostles Paul and John confronted these two issues concerning God's grace.

What shall we say, then? Shall we go on sinning, so that grace may increase? By no means! ***We died to sin; how can we live in it any longer?*** (Romans 6:1-2).

No-one who is born of God will continue to sin, because God's seed remains in him; ***he cannot go on sinning, because he has been born of God*** (1 John 3:9).

Paul and John approach the subject of sin by stating that it is 'unnatural' for a Christian to purposely choose to sin– *because God's seed remains in us* (1 John 3:9). This does not mean that a Christian never sins, as John points out.

If anybody does sin, *we have one who speaks to the Father in our defence –* ***Jesus Christ, the Righteous One. He is the atoning sacrifice for our sins***, *and not only for ours but also for the sins of the whole world* (1 John 2:1-2).

The Lord Jesus said – *"If you love me, you will obey what I command"* (John 14:15). This means that it is 'normal behaviour' for a believer to obey Him. It is not something that is forced upon us, or we reluctantly do. It is the complete opposite. We respond to His love and grace by desiring to obey His Word.

CONFESSING SIN

*If we confess our sins, He is faithful and just and **will forgive us** and purify us from all unrighteousness* (1 John 1:9).

The reason that a born-again believer confesses their sin is because it is important that we recognise those times when we have strayed away from God's principles in His Word. We do not wish to *grieve the Holy Spirit* (Eph. 4:30), who *lives in us* (John 14:17). The closer that we walk according to His ways, the more sensitive we become to thought patterns or behaviour which grieve His Spirit. We instinctively feel unease within us until we acknowledge our wrong, and at the same time change.

We confess sin not to have it forgiven, as if to 'clear the slate' once again. God does not keep a 'database' of our sins – **Blessed is the man whose sin the Lord will never count against him** (Rom. 4:8). We confess sin out of respect and reverence to our Father. We reveal our desire to change, to be like Him.

John goes on to say that if anyone does sin; we have *Jesus Christ, the Righteous One – the atoning sacrifice for our sins* (1 John 2:2). God's Word states that the Lord died once, and dealt with sin – *We have been made holy through the sacrifice of the body of Jesus Christ **once for all*** (Heb. 10:10). God is *faithful and just to forgive us* because of what Christ did for us.

If sin were to be held against a born-again believer we would be continually in and out of salvation, because it was sin that caused a barrier between us and God, until Jesus *reconciled* our relationship with Him by His sacrificial death on the Cross.

If sin was still a barrier, it would mean that we would be unsure of our relationship with the Lord. It would create huge uncertainty because we would not know if we had confessed every single sin. This would apply to each day of our life.

PUTTING OFF

> *You were taught, with regard to your former way of life, to **put off your old self**, which is being corrupted by its deceitful desires; to be made new in the attitude of your minds* (Ephesians 4:22-23).

Notice that Paul refers to the *former way of life*. He emphasises that there is a definite change that occurs when we are born again. Our *desires* (Eph. 4:22) take a different direction. They are no longer centred on ourselves. Our focus becomes – *Your Kingdom come, your will be done on earth as it is in Heaven* (Matt. 6:10).

The way in which we *put off our old self* is clearly stated – *we are made new in the attitude of our minds* (Eph. 4:22-23). There are no short cuts; it is an ongoing process. Paul gave some examples of things that we *put off*:

> ***Put off*** *falsehood and speak truthfully...control anger; do not give the devil a foothold; stop theft; unwholesome talk; get rid of all bitterness, rage and anger, brawling and slander, along with every form of malice; unforgiveness...sexual immorality; impurity; obscenity; foolish talk; coarse joking; greed* (Ephesians 4:25-5:6).

In the middle of the above list Paul explains that the consequence of committing such actions is that we – *grieve the Holy Spirit of God, with who we were sealed* (Eph. 4:30).

In order to *be made new in the attitude of our minds* we need to control what we think about each day. A person does not sin without first thinking about it. It is therefore important that we train ourselves in *capturing our thoughts* (2 Cor. 10:5), and are – ***transformed by the renewing of our mind*** (Rom. 12:1-2). As we daily *put off* our old life we make room to *put on* the new.

PUTTING ON

Put on the new self*, created to be like God in true righteousness and holiness* (Ephesians 4:24).

The above verse reveals that our new self is – *created to be like God in true righteousness and holiness*. The new self is created inside us – *If anyone is in Christ, he is a **new creation**; the old has gone, the new has come!* (2 Cor. 5:17).

We can only *put on* (Eph. 4:24) that which is already in our possession. The *new self* is the divine nature that we *participate in* (2 Peter 1:4) when Christ comes into our life by His Spirit. The sin nature is cut off, *circumcised by Christ* (Col. 2:11). Our spirit is *made alive with (His) righteousness* (Rom. 8:10).

All that remains in us is the influence that our old sin nature had over our human nature in our soul. As we *put off* that influence, and *put on the new self* that we have in our spirit, our soul changes more and more into the image of Christ.

We...are being transformed into His likeness with ever-increasing glory*, which comes from the Lord, who is the Spirit* (2 Corinthians 3:18).

Ephesians 4:24 states that the *new self* has *true righteousness and holiness*. This is Christ's righteousness and holiness. Because we have received of His divine nature within us (2 Peter 1:4), we are able to *put on* and *clothe ourselves* in His ways.

Therefore, as God's chosen people, holy and dearly loved, **clothe yourselves** *with compassion, kindness, humility, gentleness and patience. Bear with each other and forgive whatever grievances you may have against one another. Forgive as the Lord forgave you. And over all these virtues **put on love*** (Colossians 3:12-14).

CHAPTER SIX

FORGIVEN – THE FRUIT OF CHANGE

*I preached that they should **repent and turn to God and prove their repentance by their deeds*** (Acts 26:20).

When we seek God's salvation we confess our sin. We acknowledge that we have done wrong – *All have sinned and fall short of the glory of God* (Rom. 3.23). Realization that we have sinned is the first step. We then state our need and desire that Christ Jesus becomes our Saviour – *If you confess with your mouth, "Jesus is Lord," and believe in your heart that God raised Him from the dead, you will be saved* (Rom. 10:9). We repent of our sin and turn to God. Repentance (Greek – 'metanoia') means change of mind – go in another direction.

*Repent, then, and turn to God, so that **your sins may be wiped out*** (Acts 3:19).

When we are born again our sins are *wiped out*. The 'slate' is not merely wiped clean, only until the next time that we sin; instead, it is destroyed. We are *saved completely* (Heb. 7:25); we obtain *eternal redemption* (Heb. 9:12).

Confession and repentance do not stop at our salvation. The acknowledgement of wrong, coupled with a change of mind to go in another direction remain in us. The essential difference is that, after we are born again, we are in continual relationship with the Father, through Christ, by the Spirit. Sin causes offense to God, but it does not result in separation – *This is how we know that He (Christ) lives in us: we know it by the Spirit He gave us* (1 John 3:24) – *Never will I leave you* (Heb. 13:5).

We confess and repent of sin after being saved because we seek to grow more into the image of Christ (2 Cor. 3:18), and we do not want to *grieve the Holy Spirit* (Eph. 4:30).

SELF-EXAMINATION

Each one should test his own actions (Galatians 6:4).

For a Christian, self-examination is not meant to be just about self. It is about how we are changing into the image of the Lord Jesus. If it is done according to Godly principles, it will enable us to check if we are living according to God's Word, and that we are sensitive to the leading and guiding of the Spirit.

The mistake that can be made with self-examination is that it can create a works and performance mentality. If we consider that we are doing well, we can become proud of our achievements. Alternatively, if we feel that we are not measuring up to a certain standard, then guilt and condemnation can set in. Both of these sets of circumstances are counter-productive to us becoming more like the Lord. Paul warned the Galatian Church:

Are you so foolish? After beginning with the Spirit, are you now trying to attain your goal by human effort? (Gal. 3:3).

The Psalmist revealed the means by which we avoid sin – ***I have hidden your Word in my heart*** that I might not sin against you (Psalm 119:11). Jesus told His disciples how the Word and the Holy Spirit function together, so that we grow to be more like the Lord – *The Counsellor, the Holy Spirit, whom the Father will send in my name,* **will teach you all things and will remind you of everything I have said to you** (John 14:26).

Paul's chief desire in life was to grow in relationship with the Lord – *I want to know Christ* (Phil. 3:10). When we *set our heart and mind on Christ* (Col. 3:1-2), we discover that the closer that we walk with the Lord, the greater becomes our sensitivity to those things that would hinder that relationship. The intimacy with Him causes us to confess and repent of any sin far more than if we are trying to keep up a certain standard.

ATTITUDE OF MIND AND HEART

The Word of God *is living and active. Sharper than any double-edged sword, it penetrates even to dividing soul and spirit...**it judges the thoughts and attitudes of the heart*** (Hebrews 4:12).

After we are born again, confession of sin is still important as an acknowledgement that we have done wrong. But there is little point in confession alone. It needs to be accompanied by repentance, meaning a change of mind and direction. If confession and repentance are not integrally linked, we will continue in the wrong attitude of mind and heart, and most likely succumb to the same sins of that which we became conscious. We will keep confessing, but not encountering real change.

The means by which we keep a right attitude in our mind and heart is explained in the above verse; the influence of *the Word of God* (Heb. 4:12) upon our life. It states that it is *living and active*. The more that we meditate upon His Word and are led by His Spirit, the more that we will be changed by the *renewing of our mind* (Rom. 12:2). It is an ongoing process.

The Word of God *penetrates even to dividing soul and spirit* (Heb. 4:12). The reason this occurs is that our spirit is the part of us where the Lord resides within us by the Holy Spirit (John 3:6). Everything that comes forth from our spirit is in accordance with the truth of God's Word.

However, our soul which consists of our mind, heart, emotions, will, conscience, temperament, character and personality is subject to changing thoughts and attitudes. We cannot rely upon our feelings in order to follow God's ways. However, when our soul is in line with our spirit, then we have the right attitude that, if we sin, our confession will be matched by a repentant heart that is willing to change direction.

THE FRUIT OF REPENTANCE

Produce fruit in keeping with repentance (Matthew 3:8).

The fruit is produced from the seed. If we are genuine in our confession and repentance, then the seeds that we sow will subsequently produce a rich crop – *fruit in keeping with repentance* (Matt. 3:8).

If we have repented, and changed in our attitude of mind and heart, then it will be seen in our actions. This does not mean that we develop a performance mentality. It simply means that true repentance will produce genuine motives – *The integrity of the upright guides them* (Prov. 11:3).

I preached that they should repent and turn to God and ***prove their repentance by their deeds*** (Acts 26:20).

One of the results of remaining unrepentant in our attitude is that we will not effectively guard ourselves against sin and its consequences. In addition, it will subsequently lead to a hardened heart – *The Holy Spirit says: "Today, if you hear His voice, do not harden your hearts"* (Heb. 3:7-8).

In the above verse (Heb. 3:7) it states – *If you hear His voice*. We hear God's voice through His Word and by His Spirit – *When He, the Spirit of truth, comes, He will guide you into all truth. He will not speak on His own;* ***He will speak only what He hears*** (John 16:13). The Word and the Spirit work together.

The evidence of a repentant, changed heart is that we are continually drawn to, and desire the Word of God.

All Scripture is God-breathed *and is useful for teaching, rebuking, correcting and training in righteousness*
(2 Timothy 3:16).

CHAPTER SEVEN

FORGIVEN – NO CONDEMNATION

There is now no condemnation for those who are in Christ Jesus*, because through Christ Jesus the law of the Spirit of life set me free from the law of sin and death* (Romans 8:1-2)

*The Spirit of life **set me free** from the law of sin and death.* But we are not *set free* to sin, as we saw in Chapter Five – *God's grace teaches us to say "No" to ungodliness* (Titus 2:11-12).

When we are born again – **we are no longer under the supervision of the Law** (Gal. 3:24-25). If we choose to live according to the *written code* (Col. 2:14), then we will experience condemnation, because we cannot have a relationship with our Father by trying to keep the Old Covenant, with its rules and regulations. This results in a works and performance mentality. We would be denying what Jesus did at the Cross.

The consequence of living with a works and performance mind-set is that we will inevitably encounter condemnation. It will not come from God; it comes from within us. It occurs because we do not live up to the expectations that we set.

If we go down the route of works and performance it will lead us to a roundabout; we will continually go round in circles. When we commit sin, we will try to earn God's favour by doing some self-imposed penance, churning it over in our minds, and condemning ourselves, all because we fix our eyes on ourselves.

We avoid condemnation by taking the route that the Lord has given us. This enables us to keep moving forward by responding to His continual grace to us. We do not take His forgiveness for granted. We live the Christ-like life that He desires of us by keeping our eyes on Him, not on ourselves. In so doing we respond to Him by living a holy life, almost automatically.

THREE CAUSES OF GUILT AND CONDEMNATION

The Lord redeems His servants; **no one will be condemned who takes refuge in Him** (Psalm 34:22).

1. *Satan, who leads the world astray...the accuser of our brothers* (Rev. 12:9-10). **The devil** has no access to a born-again believer's spirit because it is full of Christ's righteousness (Rom. 8:10). The Holy Spirit sets a seal on us (Eph. 1:13) – *No-one can snatch them out of my hand* (John 10:28). Because the devil cannot interfere with our spirit, he attacks us in our soul by putting thoughts of doubt, fear and worry into our mind, and causing us to question our identity in Christ Jesus. That is why it is so important that we know and meditate upon God's Word.

2. The second way in which a Christian receives guilt and condemnation is from **others** – *They tie up heavy loads and put them on men's shoulders* (Matt. 23:4). How is change brought about in people? It is not by *putting heavy loads on their shoulders*, using guilt and condemnation in order to get a result? If someone is coerced into action because of a feeling of guilt, or fear of condemnation, their heart will not have the right attitude. Any change will probably only be of short-term value. But, if encouragement is used instead of guilt, then a person will respond from a willing heart, producing real and lasting change.

3. The third way is when we bring it on **ourselves**. Firstly, by not living in accordance with God's Word – *Anyone who knows the good he ought to do and doesn't do it, sins* (James 4:17). We generally know when we are not doing the right thing. The Lord does not bring condemnation; we do it to ourselves. Secondly, we allow ourselves to be condemned by not believing what God's Word tells us about His forgiveness. We ought never to take His grace for granted and continue in sin. But equally, we need to know that when we fail God, He does not want us to run away from Him; He wants us to run to Him *to take refuge*.

DEFEATING THE CAUSES OF CONDEMNATION

*They overcame him (the devil) by **the Blood of the Lamb and by the word of their testimony*** (Revelation 12:11).

We saw earlier that God's Word describes Satan as the one – *who leads the whole world astray...**the accuser of our brothers*** (Rom. 12:9-10). He continually seeks to accuse and condemn us. The way to defeat him is – *By the Blood of the Lamb and the word of their testimony* (Rev. 12:11).

The devil seeks to hold us in bondage to sin and a works mentality that makes us believe that we have to 'pay a price' for our salvation and relationship with God. This is false. Jesus said of the devil – *There is no truth in him. When he lies, he speaks his native language, for he is a liar and the father of lies* (John 8:44). The truth is that we can never pay the price for our salvation. Our *eternal redemption* (Heb. 9:12) was accomplished by the Lord Jesus offering His blood for the sins of all the world.

You were redeemed...with the precious blood of Christ, *a lamb without blemish or defect* (1 Peter 1:18-19).

At the same time as having the assurance of *the Blood of the Lamb* establishing our eternal redemption, we also speak *the word of our testimony* (Rev. 12:11). We do this by proclaiming the sure knowledge of our identity in Christ. Jesus said – ***If you hold to my teaching***, *you are really my disciples. Then you will know the truth, and **the truth will set you free*** (John 8:31-32).

Jesus explained faith to His disciples – *If you have faith as small as a mustard seed, **you can say*** (Matt. 17:20). He has given us authority to speak in His Name (Matt. 28:18-19). We defeat the devil by standing upon the *truth* of what the *Blood of Jesus* accomplished, and **declaring** the *truth* of who we are in Him, and what we do in His Name – *the word of our testimony*.

THE PEACE OF GOD

Therefore, since we have been justified through faith, **we have peace with God through our Lord Jesus Christ** (Romans 5:1).

When we are born again, we have *peace with God*. There are two wills in operation. Firstly, God's will – *He is patient with you, not wanting anyone to perish, but* **everyone to come to repentance** (2 Peter 3:9). Secondly, our will – **everyone who calls** *on the name of the Lord will be saved* (Acts 2:21).

Living in the *peace of God* again involves God's will and ours. Firstly, God's will – *The* **peace of God***, which transcends all understanding, will guard your hearts and your minds in Christ Jesus* (Phil. 4:7). Secondly, our will – **Let the peace of Christ rule** *in your hearts, since as members of one body you were called to peace* (Col. 3:15). The peace of God will completely transform our life, if we respond to Him by *letting it*.

For a born-again believer, *peace with God* is established both for now and into eternity. But to live in the *peace of God* we have to **let** *the peace of Christ rule in our hearts* (Col. 3:15). In other words, *peace with God* is received in its entirety at our salvation. But the *peace of God* is encountered progressively as we renew our mind (Rom. 12:1-2) according to the mind of Christ (1 Cor. 2:16); apply His Word to our life (Psalm 119:11); and are led by His Spirit (John 16:13). It is an act of our will.

The peace of God overcomes condemnation. There are two parts; similar to what we just examined concerning the *Blood of the Lamb and the Word of their testimony*. There is an establishing by God, followed by a response from us. The Lord Jesus has already defeated the devil. But in order for us to see victory, we have to take the authority that the Lord has given us, and implement the *testimony* of God's peace in our lives.

CHAPTER EIGHT

FORGIVING OTHERS

*Be kind and compassionate to one another, **forgiving each other**, just as in Christ God forgave you* (Ephesians 4:32).

Over the past seven chapters we have examined God's forgiveness towards us. Having encountered His love and grace in Christ Jesus, two questions arise – Firstly, how do we implement it in our life; secondly, how do we reveal it to others?

God's divine nature is revealed in one statement – *God is love* (1 John 4:8). Everything about Him flows from this truth – *Dear friends, let us love one another, for **love comes from God*** (1 John 4:7). Our interaction with people can be challenging. But we not called to like everyone; we are called to love them.

1 Corinthians 13 describes aspects of love – *Love is patient, love is kind...not easily angered, it keeps no record of wrongs...it always protects, always trusts, always hopes, always perseveres...never fails.* Each of these characteristics reveals part of God's divine nature. When we are born again, we receive of His nature within us when Christ's presence comes into us by the Holy Spirit. Because we have His love on the inside of us, every Christian has the capacity to love with the love of God.

We love because God first loved us*. If anyone says, "I love God," yet hates his brother, he is a liar. For anyone who does not love his brother, whom he has seen, cannot love God, whom he has not seen. And He has given us this command:* ***Whoever loves God must also love his brother*** (1 John 4:19-21).

When we meditate on God's Word and discover His continual love, grace and mercy towards us, then the *fruit of the Spirit* within us (Gal. 5:22) will produce greater love for others.

Forgiving Others

CLOTHED IN COMPASSION

Bear with each other and forgive whatever grievances you may have against one another*. Forgive as the Lord forgave you* (Colossians 3:13).

Every person has the five senses of sight, hearing, feeling, touch, and taste. Scripture refers to them as carnal. When we are born again we are given what could be described as a sixth sense. We encounter the realm of the Spirit of God, and as such we are not only a living being, we also become a spiritual being because of Christ Jesus, *the life-giving Spirit* (1 Cor. 15:45). He enters us; we become a *new creation in Him* (2 Cor. 5:17).

We can love people in a natural way through our human nature, according to our natural senses. But when we are born again we are able to go beyond human love, and love others with God's love. As we saw earlier in 1 Corinthians 13, just like God, we can be *patient and keep no record of wrongs*. God's love takes us much further than human love. It goes beyond feelings.

Hebrews 5:14 states that in order to mature in the faith it necessitates that we *constantly train ourselves*. The first step is to stop churning things over in our mind. Also, we will not be able to forgive others just by relying on how we feel, because if our emotions are not harnessed by the Word and Spirit of God they will inevitably fluctuate. The way to consistently love and forgive is to *train ourselves* to *put off the old self and put on the new self* (Eph. 4:22-24), which is *the divine nature of God* (2 Peter 1:4). We can love, because His Word states – *In this world we are like Him* (1 John 4:17).

Clothe yourselves *with compassion, kindness, humility, gentleness and patience…**Forgive as the Lord forgave you***. *And over all these virtues **put on love**, which binds them all together in perfect unity* (Colossians 3:12-14).

TRUSTING OTHERS

*Now it is required that **those who have been given a trust must prove faithful*** (1 Corinthians 4:2).

God's love and grace towards us is unconditional. He forgives us, irrespective of our performance as a Christian. We cannot earn His forgiveness. Likewise, He tells us emphatically that we are to forgive others, whether or not we think they deserve it. We are not to put conditions on our willingness to forgive, and we are not to expect them to earn our forgiveness. We are called to love and forgive, just like God – *Forgive as the Lord forgave you* (Col. 3:13).

Forgiveness is different to trust. Forgiveness is an act of love that is not meant to be earned; it is unconditional. Trust is different; it is conditional; it is earned – *It is required that those who have been given a trust **must prove faithful*** (1 Cor. 4:2).

Jesus told His disciples – *If you have not been **trustworthy** in handling worldly wealth, who will trust you with true riches?* (Luke 16:11). The Lord wants to use each of us; to do *the works which God prepared in advance for us to do* (Eph. 2:10). But He will not trust us with those *true riches* until we are ready; when we have proved that we can be trusted. He forgives us if we fail Him; but it is better to prove trustworthiness.

Two examples of the difference between trust and forgiveness are as follows. If a business partner cost us a large amount of money through dishonesty or incompetence, then it is our responsibility to forgive unconditionally. But that person would need to satisfactorily prove to us that they can be entrusted with money again. Likewise, if we share a confidence with someone, and then discover that they have gossiped it to others, then we are to forgive them. But we would need to be sure that they had changed before we trust them again.

RELATIONSHIPS

If it is possible, **as far as it depends on you**, *live at peace with everyone* (Romans 12:18).

The Holy Spirit would not have directed Paul to write the above words unless it was for a reason. It is clear from this verse that there will be instances when it is not possible to *live at peace* with everyone. The key to this issue is found in the words *as far as it depends on you*.

It is true to say that there are times in life when it is better to remain quiet. But at other times, words and action are required in order that an issue is dealt with righteously. We act according to God's Word by doing that which is – *right and just and fair* (Prov. 1:3). If we have said and done everything that *is possible, as far as it depends on us, to live at peace with everyone*, even difficult family issues, then we have fulfilled what God's Word has instructed us to do. Our conscience is clear.

Jesus told His disciples – *Be as shrewd as snakes and as innocent as doves* (Matt. 10:16). In other words, just like a snake, be continually aware of what is happening around you, do not be fooled or naive; but at the same time, like a dove, be harmless, keeping a pure heart – ***Above all else, guard your heart,*** *for it is the wellspring of life* (Prov. 4:23).

We saw earlier that forgiveness and trust are two separate issues; although the best result is that we can both forgive and trust someone again. We also saw that we are called to love everyone, even those we do not particularly like. We have just seen that our Father knows that it will not always be possible to live at peace with everyone. In all these situations in life that we face, His Word and Spirit will guide us. Therefore, a Christian need never give in to pressure, guilt or condemnation to comply with what others expect. Instead, we follow the Lord's ways.

CHAPTER NINE

BELONGING

I am the vine; you are the branches. If a man remains in me and I in him, he will bear much fruit; apart from me you can do nothing (John 15:5).

When we are born again, the Lord comes to live within us by the Holy Spirit – *This is how we know that **He (Christ) lives in us**; we know it by the Spirit He gave us* (1 John 3:24). We become one with the Lord – *He who unites himself with the Lord is **one with Him in spirit*** (1 Cor. 6:17). We **belong** to Him.

Have you ever wondered how close our relationship is with the Lord? *Jesus said, "If anyone loves me, he will obey my teaching. My Father will love him, and **we will come to him and make our home with him**"* (John 14:23).

He has made us a promise – *Never will I leave you; never will I forsake you* (Heb. 13:5). His Spirit is not in and out of us. He has made His position perfectly clear in His Word; He is committed to us forever.

Belonging to the Lord means that we are able to hear His voice – *He who **belongs** to God hears what God says* (John 8:47). We hear Him through His Word, and His Spirit who lives in us – *He (Spirit) will speak only what He hears* (John 16:13).

Our relationship with the Lord is not formal; it is intimate. The Song of Songs is a prophetic message of the relationship between Christ Jesus and His Church – *I **belong** to my lover (Christ), and His desire is for me* (Song of Songs 7:10).

Belonging to Christ means that we also belong to all other born-again believers – *In Christ we who are many form one body, and each member **belongs** to all the others* (Rom. 12:5).

LIFE-GIVING SPIRIT

*The first man Adam became a living being; the last Adam (Christ), **a life-giving spirit** (1 Corinthians 15:45).*

Christianity is unique. It is not a set of beliefs. It is a relationship. We **belong** to the One who is the life-giver.

*I am the Alpha and the Omega, the Beginning and the End. To him who is thirsty **I will give to drink without cost from the spring of the water of life** (Revelation 21:6).*

Our natural birth made us a descendant of Adam; our spiritual birth makes us a descendant of Jesus. When we are saved we become part of a new bloodline, because we are born again from above (1 Cor. 15:48-49). We become *a new creation in Christ* (2 Cor. 5:17).

We do not just come into newness of life. We literally receive 'The Life' within us – *Jesus said, "I am the way and the truth and **the life**"* (John 14:6).

*To all who received Him, to those who believed in His name, He gave the right to become children of God – children born not of natural descent, nor of human decision or a husband's will, but **born of God** (John 1:12-13).*

Our new birth is of the Spirit – *Flesh gives birth to flesh, but the (Holy)Spirit **gives birth** to (our) spirit* (John 3:6).

We **belong** to God – He gives spiritual birth to us. Everything about our new life, the *new creation* that we experience, has its root in the Lord Jesus – *the **firstborn** over all creation* (Col. 1:15). Jesus is *the **firstborn** among many brothers* (Rom. 8:29). He is the beginning of a new line of people. When we are born again we literally become a descendant of His.

Belonging

THE BREAD OF LIFE

Jesus said, "The bread of God is He who comes down from Heaven and **gives life to the world***" (John 6:33).*

When we accept Jesus as our Saviour we do not become part of a religious system. We **belong** to the One who is *life* itself. Being born again is a finished act. But there is also an ongoing process as we daily feed upon the Lord in order to grow and mature in Him. We do this through His Word and Spirit.

Jesus declared, "I am the bread of life" (John 6:35).

When those present questioned Jesus as to the above statements, He re-emphasised them.

Whoever eats my flesh, and drinks my blood **has eternal life***...Just as the living Father sent me and I live because of the Father, so* **the one who feeds on me will live because of me** *(John 6:54-57).*

Jesus was obviously not saying that we physically eat and drink of Him. He was emphasising to those present that **belonging** to Him is not a set of beliefs that we adhere to. Being in relationship with Him is serious, not something light or superficial. To paraphrase the above verses (John 6:54-57), Jesus was saying:

'If you want to know the meaning of life I am the answer. If you accept me into your life, and feed on my Word, you will know what it really means to live. If you fail to do so you will miss the whole point of life itself, which is to know me.'

Belonging to the Lord means that we have the life-giver, the Bread of Life in us, by His Spirit. Jesus said, *"I have come that* **that they may have life**, *and have it to the full" (John 10:10).*

LIVING WATER

*Jesus answered the Samaritan woman, "If you knew the gift of God and who it is that asks you for a drink, you would have asked Him and **He would have given you living water**"* (John 4:10).

The Holy Spirit is that *living water* (John 4:10) within us. He is not water that is still, or becomes lifeless. He is springing up and flowing. Jesus said, *"The water I give him will become in him **a spring of water** welling up to eternal life"* (John 4:14).

*Jesus said, "Whoever believes in me, as the Scripture has said, **streams of living water will flow from within him**." By this He meant the Spirit* (John 7:38-39).

When Jesus said, *"I am the vine; you are the branches"* (John 15:5), it gives the picture of life flowing from the roots through the stem and into the branches. The images that Jesus gave of the branches attached to the *vine*, the *bread* and the *living water* are all related to the sustenance that the Lord gives us. He cares for us – *His divine power has given us **everything we need** for life and Godliness* (2 Peter 1:3).

We **belong** to the Lord – *we are one with Him in spirit* (1 Cor. 6:17).

Our bodies are mortal; they will die and decay. But our spirit is eternal. It has been made alive through Christ Jesus entering into our bodies, by His Spirit, into our spirit – *Your spirit is alive because of (His) righteousness* (Rom. 8:10).

*If the Spirit of Him who raised Jesus from the dead is living in you, He who raised Christ from the dead will also give life to your mortal bodies **through His Spirit, who lives in you*** (Romans 8:11).

CHAPTER TEN

SEED

Jesus said, "This is the meaning of the Parable (of the Sower): **The seed is the Word of God**" (Luke 8:11).

The Parable of the Sower was the first parable that Jesus told. When His twelve disciples questioned Him as to the meaning, the Lord said to them – *"Don't you understand this parable? How then will you understand any parable?"* (Mark 4:13). In other words, this parable is the foundational one.

Jesus emphasised the importance of understanding that - *The seed is the Word of God* (Luke 8:11). Jesus was giving revelation to His disciples that He is that *seed*, the Word of God, manifested in the flesh - *In the beginning was the Word, and the Word was with God, and the Word was God* (John 1:1).

The Lord revealed to His disciples that if people receive that *seed* into their lives; who He is and what the Word declares about Him; it will produce true life within them - *This we proclaim concerning* **the Word of life** (1 John 1:1-2).

Our natural birth is triggered when the seed of the man is implanted into the egg of the woman. Our spiritual birth occurs by the Holy Spirit implanting the seed of life (Jesus) into our spirit. We are born again with the *imperishable seed of God*.

You have been born again, not of perishable seed, but of **imperishable (seed), through the living and enduring Word of God** (1 Peter 1:23).

The *imperishable seed* is the Word of God – *The Word become flesh (Jesus) making His dwelling among us* (John 1:14). It is only through the Lord Jesus coming into our life that we can be born again, and thereby come into relationship with God.

IMPERISHABLE SEED

*The Lord God told the serpent (Satan)... I will put enmity between you and the woman, and **between your offspring (seed) and hers**; He (Christ Jesus) will crush your head, and you will strike (bruise) His heel* (Genesis 3:14-15).

Moses, who wrote Genesis, was given revelation of Christ Jesus, The *Seed*, who was to come thousands of years later.

Genesis 3:15 reveals that the devil will bruise the Lord Jesus in His humanity – the *seed* of the woman. But although He will be bruised, the Lord will crush Satan's head, meaning his authority. This occurred at the Cross.

Having disarmed the powers and authorities, He (Christ Jesus) made a public spectacle of them, triumphing over them by the Cross (Colossians 2:15).

The Lord Jesus is – *The firstborn of many brothers* (Rom. 8:29). We are His offspring. We are of The *Seed* – Christ. Every born-again believer has partaken of the ***imperishable (seed), through the living and enduring Word of God*** (1 Peter 1:23).

You are the body of Christ, and each one of you is a part of it (1 Corinthians 12:27).

Having failed with the Lord Jesus, the devil now seeks to strike (bruise) the offspring of the Lord – His body, the Church.

Genesis 3:15 states that the devil has seed. We all face situations when the devil seeks to bruise us. But we have the authority in the Lord to overcome him. We do so through the *seed*, the Word of God. We are able to because the *seed* of Christ is greater than Satan's seed – ***The One (Christ) who is in you is greater*** *than the one (devil) who is in the world* (1 John 4:4).

Seed

THE ROOT

I, Jesus, have sent my angel to give you this testimony for the churches. **I am the Root and the Offspring of David**, *and the bright Morning Star* (Revelation 22:16).

The Lord Jesus is referred to as the *Root and offspring of David* (Rev. 5:5; 22:16), and also the *Root of Jesse* (Isaiah 11:1; 11:10; Rom. 15:12), who was King David's father. God made a covenant of everlasting Kingship and Kingdom with David (2 Sam. 7:11-16), which was a statement of the coming Messiah, who is Christ Jesus. But the Lord is also identified with Jesse, who was of humble position. It reveals that Christ has all authority, but uses it with humility.

*Who, being in the very nature God...made Himself nothing, taking the very nature of a servant...**He humbled Himself*** (Philippians 2:6-8).

The Lord is referred to as the *Lion* (Rev. 5:5). The characteristics of a lion are its majesty and strength, indicating royalty and rule. Christ is also called the *Lamb of God* (John 1:29; 1 Peter 1:19); revealing a submissive attitude, a lowly position; the nature and character of Christ's sacrifice. The Lord encompasses authority and humility.

Jesus gave us the pattern of how to live; with authority, but accompanied by a humble attitude. If the two characteristics get out of balance there are consequences. If we over-emphasise authority it will result in us becoming over-bearing; over-emphasis on humility and we will become fearful of taking authority. The two need to be balanced, to go hand-in-hand. Paul explained our response in his letter to the Philippians (2:5-11).

Your attitude should be the same as that of Christ Jesus (Philippians 2:5).

SACRIFICE

*I tell you the truth, unless a grain of wheat falls to the ground and dies, it remains only a single seed. But **if it dies, it produces many seeds*** (John 12:24).

When Jesus was explaining His death to His disciples, He referred to Himself as a *seed* falling to the ground and dying.

Jesus is that *seed* who was willing to sacrifice Himself – *to fall to the ground and die* (John 12:24). He is the Word become flesh, who came from Heaven to earth to bring us into intimate relationship with God through His sacrificial death on the Cross.

Jesus is the *seed that fell to the ground and died*. Natural seed dies, but then comes up from the ground, producing fruit. Likewise, Jesus died *on the ground* and then rose from death, creating life in those who receive Him into their life by faith.

Everyone plants 'seed' of some kind. The manner in which we live is determined by the seeds that we sow into the different areas of our life, in order to fulfil our expectations. Before becoming a Christian, the seeds that we plant into our own life are our hopes and aspirations; our dreams of what we want to see happen in our future. Those seeds reveal our own agenda.

After we are born again, we change our self-seeking attitude – **through the living and enduring Word of God** (1 Peter 1:23). That *seed* within us changes the way that we think and view our future. We do not focus upon ourselves – *We offer our bodies as a living sacrifice* (Rom. 12:1), which is a continual process.

It is no longer 'my kingdom come.' It now becomes:

Your Kingdom come, *your will be done on earth as it is in Heaven* (Matthew 6:10).

CHAPTER ELEVEN

SEED FAITH - ROOTS

By grace you have been saved, through faith *– and this not from yourselves, it is the gift of God – not of works so that no-one can boast* (Ephesians 2:8-9).

We receive the *imperishable seed* (1 Peter 1:23) **by faith** *– not of works so that no-one can boast* (Eph. 2:8-9). God's Word states – *The righteous shall live by faith* (Hab. 2:4; Rom. 1:17).

Abraham was given insight into the covenant promise of the forthcoming Saviour, Christ Jesus – *The promise comes* **by faith, so that it may be by grace** (Rom. 4:16).

The promises were spoken to Abraham and ***to his seed****. The Scripture does not say "and to seeds," meaning many people, but **"and to your seed," meaning one person, who is Christ*** (Galatians 3:16).

We can only be made righteous (right-standing with God) by receiving that *seed* into our life by faith. We cannot stand before God based upon any merit of our own. It is not by good works, our self-righteousness, or by trying to keep the Law.

What, then, was the purpose of the Law? It was added because of transgressions ***until the Seed to whom the promise referred had come****...The Law was put in charge to lead us to Christ that we might be **justified by faith***. *Now that faith has come, we are no longer under the supervision of the Law* (Galatians 3:19; 24-25).

When we are born again, Christ Jesus *The Seed* comes within us. He places His own righteousness inside us – *God made Him (Jesus) who had no sin to be sin for us, so that* ***in Him we might become the righteousness of God*** (2 Cor. 5:21).

FULLNESS

God was pleased to have **all His fullness dwell in Him** *(Christ Jesus)* (Colossians 1:19).

Jesus, whilst on earth, was both divine and human. Within His human body He had dwelling within Him – *all His (Father's) fullness* (Col. 1:19).

Through Jesus' finished work on the Cross, He has reconciled God and man. Reconciled means - two parties that were once apart through enmity, have now been brought together in friendship. Sin, which created that enmity, no longer causes a barrier between us. This occurred because of Jesus – *making peace through His blood, shed on the Cross* (Col. 1:20).

The result of being in relationship with the Father is that, through Christ Jesus, He now places *His fullness* within every born-again believer.

In Christ all the fullness of the Deity lives in bodily form, and **you have been given fullness in Christ**, *who is Head over every power and authority* (Colossians 2:9-10).

The effect of receiving *His fullness* within us is that we always have the capacity to draw from that *fullness* in whatever situation that we face in life. We do not obtain small or half-measures; nor do we have it in instalments; we receive *fullness*.

Jesus was both divine and human. He makes us like Him. Because His Spirit is in every-one who is born-again, we have *participated in* His divine nature within our human body. We receive the *fullness* of His Presence within us - **His divine power has given us everything we need** *for life and Godliness...so that* **you may participate in the divine nature** (2 Peter 1:3-4).

ROOTED

*I pray that you, **being rooted** and established in love, may have power, together with all the saints, to grasp how wide and long and high and deep is the love of Christ, and to know this love that surpasses knowledge – **that you may be filled to the measure of all the fullness of God*** (Ephesians 3:17-19).

We comprise of three parts – *spirit, soul and body* (1 Thess. 5:23). It is our spirit that is born again – *The (Holy) Spirit gives birth to (our) spirit* (John 3:6). It is that part of us that experiences the Presence of Jesus entering us by the Holy Spirit – ***Your spirit is alive because of (Christ's) righteousness*** (Rom. 8:10). It is *sealed* by the Holy Spirit entering us (Eph. 1:13).

*If the Spirit of Him who raised Jesus from the dead is living in you, He who raised Christ from the dead will also **give life to your mortal bodies through His Spirit, who lives in you*** (Romans 8:11).

The *fullness in Christ* (Col. 2:9-10) is received in our spirit, because that is where He resides in us by the Holy Spirit. That is the part of us that is born again with the ***imperishable (seed), through the living and enduring Word of God*** (1 Peter 1:23). The *Seed*, Christ Jesus, is rooted within our spirit. It is from that place within us that our spiritual growth is formed.

Our soul consists of our mind, heart, emotions, will, conscience, temperament, character and personality. When we are born again, *His fullness* does not reside in our soul, because each part of it is subject to fluctuation. But when we feed upon the *seed*, His Word, and are guided by the Holy Spirit, then our soul draws from Christ's root within our spirit, and thereby it begins to mature in the Lord so that it also becomes - ***filled to the measure of all the fullness of God*** (Eph. 3:19).

ROOTS STRENGTHENED

So then, just as you received Christ Jesus as Lord, continue to live in Him, **rooted and built up in Him, strengthened in the faith** *as you were taught, and overflowing with thankfulness* (Colossians 2:6-7).

When the *seed*, the Word of God, sprouts and grows and becomes *rooted* in the different parts of our soul, we begin to experience change. For example, our thoughts centre more upon the Lord rather than ourselves; things that we formerly worried about are no longer an issue; our motives and desires take on a different perspective. Sometimes, we do not even realise what is taking place, or how the transformation is happening within us.

This is what the Kingdom of God is like. A man scatters seed on the ground. Night and day, whether he sleeps or gets up, **the seed sprouts and grows, though he does not know how** (Mark 4:26-27).

Becoming *rooted and built up in Him*, results in us being *strengthened in the faith* (Col. 2:7). This occurs when the *seed* has gone into good soil within our soul; that which is responsive to the Word of God. Becoming strong in our faith is the direct result of sowing *seed*, which *sprouts and grows*, and takes *root*.

The importance of the *seed* going into good soil and becoming *rooted* is revealed by Jesus in the Parable of the Sower – *The one who received the seed that fell on rocky places is the man who hears the Word and at once receives it with joy. But* **since he has no root**, *he lasts only a short time* (Matt. 13:20-21).

There are no short cuts to spiritual growth. Scripture reveals a process – **First the stalk, then the ear, then the full grain in the ear** (Mark 4:28). Our response is to prepare the ground in our soul in order to receive the *seed*, the Word of God.

CHAPTER TWELVE

SEED FAITH – REPRODUCING

*God said, "Let the land produce vegetation: seed-bearing plants and trees on the land that **bear fruit with seed in it, according to their various kinds**"* (Genesis 1:11).

At creation, God created vegetation that had *seed* within it (Gen. 1:11). He did the same with living creatures (Gen. 1:21), and then with living beings (Gen. 1:28).

Everything that He created on earth had *seed* within it, in order to **reproduce** after its own kind. At creation, He placed within vegetation, living creatures, and humans, the means by which they could create life by the implanting of *seed*.

Whatever is planted will reproduce after its own kind. If we plant corn we expect a cornfield. When God created seed in vegetation, living creatures and humans He revealed a natural and a spiritual principle – seed produces fruit from what is sown.

At creation, God revealed His faith. He spoke and called things into being - *The God who gives life to the dead and **calls things that are not as though they were*** (Rom. 4:17).

When we are born again we receive of His faith – *The measure of faith God has given you* (Rom. 12:3). He has enabled every born-again believer to use that *measure of faith* to sow *spiritual seed* in order to produce life – **according to His kind**.

Take root below and bear fruit above (2 Kings 19:30).

When the seed, the Word of God, becomes *rooted* within us we will *bear fruit above*, not only in our own life and that of others, but also into those situations that we speak His Word. We will reproduce according to the *seed* that we sow.

SOWING

A man reaps what he sows (Galatians 6:7).

We continually sow seed of some kind, by our thoughts, words, and actions. What sort of harvest are we reaping?

We saw in Chapter Ten that we are born again because of The *Seed*, the Lord Jesus, entering our life. We become His offspring (Rom. 8:29) – *How great is the love the Father has lavished on us, that **we should be called children of God**! And that is what we are!* (1 John 3:1).

*To all who received Him (Christ Jesus), to those who believed in His name, **He gave the right to become children of God** – children born not of natural descent, nor of human decision or a husband's will, but **born of God*** (John 1:12).

At creation, the Lord God put in place a natural and spiritual law that ***seed*** produces after its own ***kind*** (Genesis 1:11-12; 21-22; 27-28).

That being the case, every born-again believer has the capacity within them to literally sow the *seed* of God. We are His offspring. We are of His *'kind,'* His family, because of the Lord Jesus within us, by the Holy Spirit - *He who unites himself with the Lord is one with Him in spirit* (1 Cor. 6:17).

Because He is within us, we can think like Him – *We have the mind of Christ* (1 Cor. 2:16). This is the Holy Spirit within our spirit, who *guides us into all truth* (John 16:13).

Therefore, because we can think like the Lord, we can also speak like Him - ***This is what we speak***, *not in words taught us by human wisdom but in words taught by the (Holy) Spirit* (1 Cor. 2:13).

DECLARING WHAT WE SOW

Do *not let (My Word) depart from your mouth*; *meditate on it day and night, so that you may be careful to do everything written in it. Then you will be prosperous and successful* (Joshua 1:8).

When Joshua was about to lead the Israelite nation across the Jordan to enter the Promised Land, the Lord God gave the above instruction to Joshua in order for him to experience victory.

Meditation in the above verse means to 'mutter/speak.' Joshua was successful because he did what God had instructed him to do. He *meditated* on the Word of God by speaking it into the situations that he faced. He continually planted *seed* by declaring God's purposes.

The meaning of *Seed Faith* is that we sow the *seed*, the Word of God, by speaking and declaring it into things - **calling things that are not as though they were** (Rom. 4:17).

*Jesus said, "I tell you the truth, **if you have faith and do not doubt**...**you can say** to this mountain, 'Go, throw yourself into the sea,' and it will be done"* (Matthew 21:21).

Seed faith will not produce fruit if, after planting, we dig it back up by having doubt; using negative words. There is no point in a farmer sowing seed one day, and then digging it up the next day. This sort of action will not produce a harvest.

Many times Joshua faced great difficulty. But he kept declaring the Word of God, which brought success. He both sowed and reaped. One of his last instructions was as follows:

Be careful to obey all that is written in the (Word of God), *without turning aside to the right or to the left* (Joshua 23:6).

LIFE-CHANGING SEED

Jesus said, "The words I have spoken to you are spirit and they are life" (John 6:63).

Christ Jesus, The *Seed*, is within every born-again believer. When we apply His Words, the Word of God, to our lives, it is literally life-changing. There is incredible potential within every Christian. Our response to Him is to get the *seed* rooted within us, and apply it to our lives and that of others.

Let the Word of Christ dwell in you richly (Colossians 3:16).

After Jesus had revealed Himself to the two disciples on the road to Emmaus they said to one another – *"Were not our hearts burning within us while He talked with us on the road and **opened the Scriptures to us**"* (Luke 24:32).

When we are born again we receive Christ's Anointing – *He anointed us…You have an anointing from the Holy One…The anointing you received from Him remains in you* (2 Cor. 1:21; 1 John 2:20; 27).

His divine power has given us everything we need for life and Godliness (2 Peter 1:3). We have the capacity, because of Christ's presence within us by His Spirit, to walk in close fellowship with our Father, and to experience that which is life-changing, in every aspect of our life.

Sowing seed is a spiritual principle which produces a practical application. Helping others, including financially, is part of the way that we see *increase* in both ourselves and others.

*Now He (the Father) who supplies seed to the sower and bread for food **will also supply and increase your store of seed*** (2 Corinthians 9:10).

CHAPTER THIRTEEN

SEED FAITH – SOWING & REAPING

Jesus said, "This is what the Kingdom of God is like. ***A man scatters seed on the ground****. Night and day, whether he sleeps or gets up**, the seed sprouts and grows, though he does not know how**. All by itself the soil produces corn – first the stalk, then the ear, then the full grain in the ear* (Mark 4:26-28).

Miracles such as healing, deliverance, and provision, can occur instantaneously. But there are also the acts of God that happen over time. In the above verse a process is described. The *seed* is sown; it sprouts and grows; the stalk develops; the ear is formed, and then the full grain in the ear.

Jean Giono was a novelist who wrote stories about life in Provence, France. One such story became world famous. It concerned a shepherd, Elzeard Bouffier, who each day planted acorns as he walked through his land. In time, a large forest in Provence grew from his daily planting of seed.

Although, as Giono acknowledged, the story is fictional, many people have drawn inspiration from that shepherd. Throughout such places as Africa and India, relief agencies have worked with Governments in planting forests, bringing life to areas and preventing soil erosion. Over time, millions of seeds have been planted, and the work is continuing.

If we can draw inspiration from a novelist, how much more ought we to take hold of the words that the Lord Jesus has given us. Each day we can plant *seed*, the Word of God into our life, and that of others. In the fullness of time it will bear fruit.

Now to Him who is able to do immeasurably more than all we ask or imagine (Ephesians 3:20).

FRUIT

You know that your labour in the Lord is not in vain
(1 Corinthians 15:58).

Seed faith sows for the future, even though we may never see the harvest ourselves. This is what occurred in the Samaritan village of Sychar, where Jesus and His disciples visited.

When Jesus was resting by a well in the village, He talked to a Samaritan woman who had come to draw water. He revealed to her that He gives *living water* (John 4:10). He told her things about herself, and then spoke of - *true worshippers who will worship the Father in spirit and truth* (John 4:23).

*The woman said, "**I know that Messiah** (called Christ) **is coming**. When He comes, He will explain everything to us." Jesus declared, "I who speak to you am He"* (John 4:25-26).

The names of the people who had sown *seed* into that village down through the centuries are not known. But their names are in the *Lamb's Book of life* (Rev. 21:27). They are known in Heaven. They faithfully sowed words of life and revelation. A future people experienced the fulfilment of those words. Jesus told His disciples:

One sows and another reaps**...I sent you to reap what you have not worked for. **Others have done the hard work, and you have reaped the benefits of their labour" (John 4:37).

We sow, and God produces the growth – *I (Paul) planted the seed, Apollos watered it, but **God made it grow*** (1 Cor. 3:6).

The *seed* that is planted by one generation does not die. It remains 'alive.' Likewise, prayers do not die. The prayers of past generations are still 'living' and join with those of today.

GROWTH

Jesus said, "What shall we say the Kingdom of God is like, or what parable shall we use to describe it? It is like a mustard seed, which is the smallest seed you plant in the ground. **Yet when planted, it grows and becomes the largest of all garden plants**, *with such big branches that the birds of the air can perch in its shade"* (Mark 4:30-32).

When the *seed* is rooted in us we are able to hold fast, even when there is no visible sign of breakthrough - *Faith is being sure of what we hope for and* ***certain of what we do not see*** (Heb. 11:1).

We are able to sow into the spiritual; that which is unseen with our natural eyes. Jesus said to His disciples, *"If you have faith as small as a mustard seed,* ***you can say...***" (Matt. 17:20).

Our Heavenly Father told the prophet Jeremiah that he would accomplish things through words.

I have put my words in your mouth*...I appoint you over nations and kingdoms* ***to uproot*** *and* ***tear down****, to* ***destroy*** *and* ***overthrow****, to* ***build*** *and to* ***plant*** (Jeremiah 1:9-10).

Through the words that Jeremiah spoke, he would *uproot* (bad seed); *tear down* (strongholds of sin, doubt and fear); *destroy and overthrow* (kingdoms that the devil builds); *build* (the Kingdom of God); *plant* (the good seed – the Word of God).

The tongue has the power of life and death, and those who love it will ***eat its fruit*** (Proverbs 18:21).

Something will grow from our thoughts and words – *A man reaps what he sows* (Gal. 6:7). The question we each have to ask ourselves is – What sort of fruit do I want to eat?

THANKFULNESS

So then, just as you received Christ Jesus as Lord, continue to live in Him, **rooted and built up in Him, strengthened in the faith** *as you were taught, and* **overflowing with thankfulness** (Colossians 2:6-7).

Thankfulness accompanies faith.

Joyfully giving thanks to the Father*, who has qualified you to share in the inheritance of the saints in the Kingdom of Light* (Colossians 1:12).

We become *rooted and built up in the Lord* when the *seed*, the Word of God, has gone into good soil within us. It has taken root, which results in us being *strengthened in the faith*. This is accompanied by a thankful heart. Faith and thankfulness go hand-in-hand.

Therefore, **since we are receiving a kingdom** *that cannot be shaken,* **let us be thankful** (Hebrews 12:28).

Born-again believers have been birthed into the Kingdom of God (Col. 1:12; 1 Thess. 2:12). It has also been birthed into us – *The Kingdom of God is within you* (Luke 17:21).

Throughout the Book of Isaiah there are prophetic statements about the coming Messiah, Christ Jesus. Chapter sixty-one reveals the Anointing that will be upon Him, and that His Kingdom will be seen throughout the world. The Scripture compares it to *seed* growing, producing life and praise.

For as the soil makes the young plant come up and a garden ***causes seeds to grow****, so the Sovereign Lord will make* ***righteousness and praise spring up before all nations*** (Isaiah 61:11).

CHAPTER FOURTEEN

SEED FAITH – ENDURING

Faith comes by hearing, and hearing by the Word of God (Romans 10:17 King James translation).

Faith is the door by which we enter into relationship and revelation in the Lord. The absence of faith is the reason that a generation of the Israelites failed to enter the Promised Land.

*They were not able to enter, **because of their unbelief**...The message they heard was of no value to them, because those who heard **did not combine it with faith*** (Hebrews 3:19; 4:2)

Their words of unbelief were seeds that they sowed.

*All the Israelites grumbled against Moses and Aaron, and the whole assembly said to them, "**If only we had died in Egypt! Or in this desert!**"* (Numbers 14:2).

They subsequently reaped what they had sown. They died in the desert. Their own words brought death. It did not have to have ended that way – ***The tongue has the power of life and death**, and those who love it will eat its fruit* (Prov. 18:21).

We have a choice. Do we believe the Word of God, and do as it says; or do we follow what we 'feel?' – *Anyone who listens to the Word but does not do what it says is like a man who looks at his face in a mirror and, after looking at himself, goes away and forgets what he looks like* (James 1:23-24).

It is never too late to dig up bad seed; thoughts that are planted in our mind by the devil, or those negative thoughts that we have chosen to think and say ourselves. We can replace them with the good *seed*, the Word of God, which will always overcome the bad seed (Gen. 3:15).

DIGGING UP BAD SEED

Each one is tempted when, by his own evil desire, he is dragged away and enticed. Then, **after desire has conceived, it gives birth to sin**; *and sin, when it is full-grown, gives birth to death* (James 1:14-15).

The principle of reaping the seed that we sow can be seen in our thoughts. Where we are in life, whether spiritually, emotionally, and even physically can be traced back to the seeds that we have planted in our mind and heart – *As a man thinks in his heart so he is* (Prov. 23:7 King James translation).

Sin is the result of wrong thinking. A person does not sin without first thinking about it. The above verses in James reveal the process that takes place. First comes the *desire* – that which we think about. Secondly, the desire is dwelt upon and *conceived* – its life is formed. Thirdly, it becomes rooted in our thoughts and heart, and in so doing *gives birth to the sin*. Fourthly, when it is full grown, and has been acted upon, it gives *birth to death*. Sin does not suddenly or spontaneously happen. It is produced from thoughts; seeds planted, and then conceived.

If we compare these verses in James with Mark 4:28 we will see that there is a similarity; seed planted; conceived; rooted; growing; producing fruit.

The difference is that Mark 4:28 refers to fruit in the Kingdom of God from sowing *seed*, the Word of God; whereas the verses in James warn of the danger of sowing seed that conceives sin. It can be prevented - ***I have hidden your Word in my heart that I might not sin against you*** (Psalm 119:11).

Bad seed that is sown, can become rooted, form a stalk, and then produce fruit, unless it is dug up – *See to it that...**no bitter root grows up** to cause trouble and defile many* (Heb. 12:15).

SEASONS

Preach the Word; be prepared in season and out of season (2 Timothy 4:2).

There are different seasons in life that we all encounter. Paul encouraged Timothy to sow the *seed*, the Word of God, continually, even in those times that appear to be difficult.

The words we use are powerful. They affect our present and future; *The tongue has the power of life and death* (Prov. 18:21).

Every day we use hundreds of words in our mind, and through our mouth. Where we have arrived at in life has been determined by the words that we have spoken to ourselves, or what has been said by other people that have influenced us. Those thoughts and words are the seeds that have produced a harvest of some kind. The question is: What type of seed is stored within us?

*Out of the overflow of the heart the mouth speaks. The good man brings good things out of the **good stored up in him**, and the evil man brings evil things out of the **evil stored up in him*** (Matthew 12:34-35).

When we enter a season that is stressful, difficult and challenging, the words that come out of our mouths will reveal what has been *stored* in our heart.

When we continually plant the *seed*, the Word of God, into 'good soil' within us; that which is prepared and receptive; then we will be ready for whatever we face in life. In so doing, it will produce a rich harvest in us. From that store of the Word in us, we will have a plentiful supply of *seed* to sow into other people's lives, and thereby see the Kingdom of God grow wherever we are – ***in season and out of season***.

ENDURING SEED

*We have not received the spirit of the world but the Spirit who is from God, that we may understand what God has freely given us. This is what **we speak, not in words taught us by human wisdom but in words taught by the (Holy) Spirit**, expressing spiritual truths in spiritual words*
(1 Corinthians 2:12-13).

The Word and the Spirit work together. The Spirit helps us understand and apply the Word of God to our life, and also in the way in which we speak to others – *When He, the Spirit of truth, comes, He will guide you into all truth* (John 16:13).

Jesus revealed in the 'Parable of the Sower' that the *seed is the Word of God* (Luke 8:11-15). The Lord, by His Spirit, sows *seed* into peoples' hearts.

He also sows His *seed* through us – He *sends out workers into His harvest field.* (Matt. 9:38). The *seed* is sown by us, in faith - **the living and enduring Word of God** (1 Peter 1:23). Whatever the season, the *enduring seed* that we sow will enable those who receive the *seed* to experience a rich crop.

The 'Parable of the Sower' states - *The farmer went out to sow his seed* (Luke 8:5). It was a purposeful action on his part. He was very focussed upon what he sought to achieve. It was not an occasional pastime. It was his calling - *Whatever your hand finds to do, do it with all your might* (Ecclesiastes 9:10).

'Don't judge each day by the harvest you reap, but by the seeds you plant' (Robert Louis Stevenson).

*Let us not become weary in doing good, for **at the proper time we will reap a harvest if we do not give up***
(Galatians 6:9).

CHAPTER FIFTEEN

THE KINGDOM OF GOD – HIS NATURE

The Kingdom of God is not a matter of eating and drinking, but of ***righteousness, peace and joy in the Holy Spirit*** (Romans 14:17).

When Paul wrote to the church in Rome it consisted of both Gentile and Jewish believers. The Gentiles recognised that all the laws and feasts of the Old Testament were fulfilled in Christ Jesus. Unfortunately, a number of the Jewish believers wished to hold onto certain customs and rituals, which included what they thought that they should eat and drink. This was causing disputes within their fellowship.

In the midst of this confusion, Paul, being led by the Holy Spirit, sought to bring clarity, and focus them upon what the Kingdom of God really consists of – *righteousness, peace and joy in the Holy Spirit* (Rom. 14:17).

Paul warned them against *passing judgement on disputable matters* (Rom. 14:1); the trivialities of life waste time. In addition, we are to be aware of one another – *None of us lives to himself alone* (Rom. 14:7). He was encouraging them not to get *taken captive* (Col. 2:8) by 'issues,' and self-righteous opinions.

He explained that the Kingdom of God is not about following rules and regulations imposed by man. Jesus did not come to start a religion; He came to bring us into relationship with The Father. Therefore, let us not be taken captive by 'religious traditions.'

See to it that no-one takes you captive through hollow and deceptive philosophy, which ***depends on human tradition and the basic principles of this world rather than on Christ*** (Colossians 2:8).

THE KINGDOM OF GOD IS...RIGHTEOUSNESS

There are two aspects to righteousness. Christ's righteousness is **imputed** into us when we are born again of His Spirit. His righteousness is then **imparted** by His Spirit as we live in a Godly manner through knowledge of His Word, and the leading of the Holy Spirit.

We are declared righteous (right-standing with God) because – *Our spirit is alive because of (Christ's) righteousness* (Rom. 8:10). Because of His righteousness within us, we can live a holy life – *Live self-controlled, upright and Godly lives* (Titus 2:12).

We respond to His righteousness by *the renewing of our mind* (Rom. 12:2) according to *the mind of Christ* (1 Cor. 2:16). A born-again believer cannot become more righteous in their spirit, because it contains Christ's righteousness. But our soul receives His righteousness being imparted to it as we are *transformed* (Rom. 12:2) by the Word of God and the teaching of the Holy Spirit in our mind, heart and emotions.

It is good to be inspired by the Godly living of others. Paul's life was an example to Timothy – *You know all about my teaching, my way of life, my purpose, faith, patience, love, endurance, persecutions, sufferings* (2 Tim. 3:10-11). But we cannot become more righteous than another believer, because it is Christ's righteousness alone, not ours. When His righteousness is imparted to us, as we respond to Him, it is by His Spirit, not by any 'righteousness' that we might think that we develop by our own merit.

The key to understanding righteousness is to – ***fix our eyes on Jesus**, the author and perfecter of our faith* (Heb. 12:2). Paul taught this to the believers at Rome (Rom. 14); to take our eyes off our own and other people's performances, views, traditions and customs, and fix them on The One who really matters.

THE KINGDOM OF GOD IS...PEACE

Peace means harmonious relationship. Every born-again believer has harmony with God because we have been reconciled (brought into friendship) with Him through Jesus' sacrificial death on the Cross.

Since we have been justified (acquitted from guilt) through faith, **we have peace with God through our Lord Jesus Christ**, *through whom we have gained access by faith into this grace in which we now stand* (Romans 5:1-2).

Peace in the world has a different meaning to that in the Kingdom of God. Peace in the world is dependent upon circumstances; whereas peace in the Kingdom of God is received through a Person, the Lord Jesus Christ – **He Himself is our peace** (Eph. 2:14). That is why a Christian is able to encounter a peace that is beyond human understanding.

The peace of God, which transcends all understanding, *will guard your hearts and your minds in Christ Jesus* (Philippians 4:7).

Paul walked in close relationship with the Lord. As a consequence of this he not only knew *peace with God*, but he also experienced the *peace of God*. He encouraged every believer to – **let the peace of Christ rule in your hearts**, *since as members of one body* **you were called to peace** (Col. 3:15).

When our focus is upon the Lord Jesus, who is *our peace* (Eph. 2:14), we will not waste time on issues that create disharmony within His body, the Church (Rom. 14:19).

Paul testified of the result of having *the peace of God* – *I* **have learned** *the secret of being content in any and every situation* (Phil. 4:12). He was not side-tracked by circumstances.

KINGDOM OF GOD IS…JOY IN THE HOLY SPIRIT

The world's joy is different to that of the Kingdom of God. In the world, in a similar manner to peace, joy is dependent upon circumstances. It is linked to our emotional well-being. However, a Christian's source of joy is not in their soul; it comes from their spirit, where the Holy Spirit resides within us.

*Jesus said, "Whoever believes in me, as the Scripture has said, **streams of living water will flow from within him**." By this He meant the Spirit, whom those who believed in Him were later to receive* (John 7:38-39).

Acts 16:11-40 describes Paul and Silas' imprisonment at Philippi. They had been harshly treated, but *about midnight they were praying and singing hymns to God* (Acts 16:25). Their physical circumstances were severe. But they had joy welling up from within them. How is this possible? The answer is that they had come to know that *the joy of the Lord is your strength* (Nehemiah 8:10). They knew the place in which to find that joy – *You will fill me with joy **in your presence*** (Psalm 16:11).

Joy in the Holy Spirit is revealed in how we conduct ourselves daily; our manner of living. It is experienced in widely different ways. It can be encountered in stillness; other times in extravagant worship. Sometimes it is spoken in human language; other times in tongues that the Spirit gives us – *pray in the Holy Spirit* (Jude 20). In our own expression of joy, it is important that we do not judge others as to how their joy is expressed.

Jesus rejoiced in seeing the future Kingdom that was coming through His death and resurrection – *Who for the joy set before Him endured the Cross* (Heb. 12:2). We have His joy within us.

*Remain in my love, obey my commands…**so that my joy may be in you**, and that your joy may be complete* (John 15:9-11).

CHAPTER SIXTEEN

THE KINGDOM OF GOD – A NEW BEGINNING

***Your Kingdom is an everlasting Kingdom**, and your dominion endures through all generations* (Psalm 145:13).

When we are born again we are **called into** (1 Thess. 2:12), and **brought into** the Kingdom of God.

*God has rescued us from the dominion of darkness and **brought us into the Kingdom** of the Son He loves, in whom we have redemption, the forgiveness of sins* (Colossians 1:13-14).

Notice the contrast between the two *dominions* in the above verses – *the dominion of God* (Psalm 145:13) and the *dominion of darkness* (Col. 1:13).

Before we become a Christian we may lead a moral and upright life, and have a love and concern for other people. It is obviously good to live in such a manner. But the fact remains that it is still *darkness* until we are born again. The *light* that we come into is not an abstract state; it is a relationship with the person of Christ Jesus, from whom the *light* emanates.

*"**I am the light of the world**. Whoever follows me will never walk in darkness, but will have the light of life"* (John 8:12).

The *Kingdom* that we are 'born into' is full of light – *to share in the inheritance of the saints in the **Kingdom of light*** (Col. 1:12). It is only possible to understand the life and principles in that Kingdom through *The Light* – Christ Jesus. The Holy Spirit who is *in us* (John 14:17), enables us to 'see' everything in God's Kingdom through The Light – *We have received the Spirit who is from God, that **we may understand** what God has freely given us* (1 Cor. 2:12).

NEW CLOTHES FOR THE KINGDOM

Put on the new self, which is being renewed in knowledge in the image of its Creator (Colossians 3:10).

Immediately upon entering the Kingdom of God we are given a 'new set of clothes.' These are the righteousness and divine nature of Christ Jesus that He imputes into our spirit by the Holy Spirit – *Your spirit is alive because of (His) righteousness* (Rom. 8:10).

*May your priests be **clothed with righteousness*** (Psalm 132:9).

*I delight greatly in the Lord; my soul rejoices in my God. For He has **clothed me with garments of salvation** and **arrayed me in a robe of righteousness*** (Isaiah 61:10).

The new clothes – *the righteousness of Christ Jesus* (Rom. 8:10) – enable us to always enter the presence of our Heavenly Father, irrespective of how we may 'feel' on any particular day. It is the receiving of His 'clothes' that gives us the position of a *royal priesthood* (1 Peter 2:9) within His Kingdom.

Having received His 'clothes,' the Lord wants us to *put off our old self* in order to *put on the new self, created to be like God in true righteousness and holiness* (Eph. 4:22-24). The 'new wardrobe' we receive is extensive. He wants us to 'wear' all that He has given us, so that we are recognised as believers.

The new self is received in our spirit, which is the part of us that is born again – *The (Holy) spirit gives birth to (our) spirit* (John 3:6). If we endeavour to live in the Kingdom of God still wearing 'clothes' from our *old self*, then people will not recognise us as a Christian. He has *clothed us with His garments* so that we can reveal His salvation to the world.

A NEW LANGUAGE FOR THE KINGDOM

This is what we speak, not in words taught us by human wisdom but in words taught by the Spirit, ***expressing spiritual truths in spiritual words*** (1 Corinthians 2:13).

When we are born again, we begin to learn a new language, which is according to God's Word, rather than *conforming to the pattern of this world* (Rom. 12:2). Our thoughts begin to change, because our natural mind begins to be *transformed* by *the mind of Christ* (1 Cor. 2:16), which is the Holy Spirit within our spirit, revealing the Lord's words and direction. The result of *our mind being renewed* (Rom 12:2), is that our conversation changes – *Out of the overflow of the heart the mouth speaks* (Matt. 12:34).

This does not mean that we speak in religious clichés, or continually quote Scripture to people. It simply means that the inward change that is taking place in our mind, heart and emotions is expressed in our words and conversation; our talk becomes more meaningful. We have a Kingdom view of matters.

In order to 'explore' the Kingdom of God we need to learn that new language. The 'information and direction signs' that we 'see' in His Kingdom are written by the Holy Spirit, according to God's Word. The Word and the Spirit function together, confirming one another. If we do not read the signs that God places for us, there is a danger that we will go round in circles.

It is God's desire that we become fluent in His language, possessing a 'large vocabulary' according to His Word. One of the key changes that become noticeable to others is that we talk less about ourselves and more of the Lord, and His Kingdom.

We discover that words are powerful. That is why we *guard our heart* (Prov. 4:23) in order to express positive words – ***The tongue has the power of life and death*** (Prov. 18:21).

A NEW CURRENCY FOR THE KINGDOM

Without faith it is impossible to please God (Hebrews 11:6).

When we enter the Kingdom of God, not only are we given new clothes and a new language, but we are also given a new currency. Our old currency prior to becoming a Christian was works. When we are born again we receive a new currency, namely *faith*. Every believer is given this currency – *The measure of faith God has given you* (Rom. 12:3). It is free. Jesus has already paid the price (Rom. 5:17).

> *Come, all you who are thirsty, come to the waters; and you who have no money, come, buy and eat! Come,* **buy wine and milk without money and without cost** (Isaiah 55:1).

Prior to being saved, our mind-set was that of works and performance. We tried to earn favour with people. But, in God's Kingdom there are a different set of principles. Everything we receive is because of God's grace, through faith – *By grace you have been saved,* ***through faith…not by works*** (Eph. 2:8-9).

Our works are the product of faith – ***Your work produced by faith*** (1 Thess. 1:3).

Our old 'currency' is of no value in the Kingdom of God. The reason being is that it is carnal, which means according to our five senses – that which we see, hear, touch, feel and smell. When we are born again we receive a 'sixth sense,' because of the Holy Spirit within us, who leads and guides us in our faith.

Our new 'currency' of faith grows as we use it. The more we 'spend,' the more we receive – *Your faith is growing more and more* (2 Thess. 1:3). Faith comes from the Word of God (Rom. 10:17). It grows by investing it; being put into action – *Faith by itself, if it is not accompanied by action, is dead* (James 2:17).

CHAPTER SEVENTEEN

THE KINGDOM OF GOD – A NEW LIFE

The Kingdom of God is within (in the midst of) you
(Luke 17:21).

'Kingdom' (basileia) has the meaning of – sovereignty, royal power and dominion. The literal meaning of the above verse is – 'where the King is, there is the Kingdom.'

His Kingdom is where the King (Christ Jesus) is given rightful rule and authority. It occurs in us when we respond to the *calling* (1 Thess. 2:12) by the Holy Spirit. We are *brought into* (Col. 1:13) the Kingdom of God; at the same time we receive the Kingdom when Christ Jesus enters our spirit by the Holy Spirit. He establishes His Kingdom rule (Luke 17:21). Our spirit is sealed by the Spirit (Eph. 1:13). The devil has no access.

The Lord wants to establish His Kingdom principles not only in our spirit, but in all of our life. We comprise of *spirit, soul and body* (1 Thess. 5:23). Our soul consists of our mind, heart, emotions, will, conscience, temperament, character and personality. When we renew our mind according to *the mind of Christ* (1 Cor. 2:16), which is the Holy Spirit, then we are continually establishing His Kingdom. Not only does this affect us on our inside, but it also enables us to move in His authority.

The Kingdom of God is not a matter of talk but of power
(1 Cor. 4:20).

Every born-again believer is **called**, **brought into**, and **receives** the Kingdom. We then learn to **live in** that Kingdom through His Word and Spirit – *His divine power has given us everything we need for life and Godliness* (2 Peter 1:3). His Holy Spirit reveals *His very great and precious promises* through His Word, as we *participate in the divine nature* (2 Peter 1:4).

A NEW WAY OF UNDERSTANDING

We have not received the spirit of the world but the Spirit who is from God, **that we may understand** *what God has freely given us* (1 Corinthians 2:12).

When we are born again our *understanding* of things change, because of the Holy Spirit within us. We can only understand the Kingdom of God through the Spirit.

Prior to becoming a Christian we used worldly logic and reason in our natural mind in our soul, in order to understand. There is nothing wrong with making judgements in this manner. But when we enter the Kingdom of God we discover that it does not operate according to the world's principles. This does not mean that we abandon logic and reason. It simply means that, having *the mind of Christ* (Holy Spirit) within us, we have the ability to see things in a different perspective, in faith – 'Reason can only go so far, whereas faith has no limits' (Pascal).

A person needs the Holy Spirit in order to understand the Word of God; the reason being that the natural mind cannot comprehend the spiritual.

The man without the Spirit does not accept the things that come from the Spirit of God, for they are foolishness to him, and **he cannot understand them, because they are spiritually discerned** (2 Corinthians 2:14).

Old Testament believers had revelation, and knew the Holy Spirit with them; but New Testament believers have something greater; the Spirit **within** them – *He lives with you and will be* ***in you*** (John 14:17). That is why Paul, under the inspiration of the Spirit, added to what Isaiah said (Isaiah 64:4) – *No mind has conceived what God has prepared for those who love Him,* **but God has revealed it to us by His Spirit** (1 Cor. 2:9-10).

A NEW WAY OF LIVING

I urge you, in view of God's mercy, to **offer your bodies as living sacrifices**, *holy and pleasing to God – this is your spiritual act of worship* (Romans 12:1).

Jesus told us – *I have come that they may have life, and have it to the full* (John 10:10). In order to live life to the full in the Kingdom of God we are called to die to ourselves.

Jesus said to His disciples, "If anyone would come after me, **he must deny himself and take up his cross and follow me**. *For whoever wants to save his life will lose it, but whoever loses his life for me will find it"* (Matthew 16:24-25).

Dealing with our ego-self is probably the area that causes the most conflict within us. It reveals whether we are living with one foot in our old kingdom, and one foot within the Kingdom of God. When we are born again, we become *one in spirit* (1 Cor. 6:17) with the Lord Jesus within our spirit; we are fully within His Kingdom in respect of our salvation. But our human nature within our soul can still revert to 'old ways.'

Self-centredness is a killer. It prevents us from developing a close relationship with the Lord. If it persists, we will be unable to hear His voice through His Word and Spirit, because our thoughts and emotions revolve around ourselves. Our focus becomes 'How does this affect me,' rather than focussing upon the Lord – **Your Kingdom come, your will be done** (Matt. 6:10).

Scripture reveals that King Saul's focus was upon himself – *He set up a monument in his own honour* (1 Sam. 15:12); whereas Noah maintained humility. Upon leaving the Ark, the first thing he did was to *build an altar to the Lord* (Gen. 8:20). Each day there is a question we all face – whose kingdom am I building? We can either be a Saul or a Noah – the choice is ours.

THE KINGDOM OF HEAVEN

Jesus said, "I say to you that many will come from the east and the west, and will take their places at the feast with Abraham, Isaac and Jacob in **the Kingdom of Heaven**" (Matthew 8:11).

The Kingdom of God and the Kingdom of Heaven are used interchangeably in Scripture, although sometimes they refer to different aspects of His one Kingdom.

His Kingdom has already come, as revealed in the Lord Jesus' incarnate birth and ministry. John the Baptist prepared the way for Him declaring, *"Repent, for the Kingdom of Heaven is near"* (Matt. 3:2). When Jesus began ministering He preached – *"Repent, for the Kingdom of Heaven is near"* (Matt. 4:17).

The Kingdom of God continues to come as we do *His will on earth as it is in Heaven* (Matt. 6:10). We do so by establishing the Lord Jesus as King in our lives, and in all of life's circumstances, so that He has the supremacy.

> *He is the head of the body, the church; he is the beginning and the firstborn from among the dead, so that* **in everything He might have the supremacy** (Colossians 1:18).

There is a future Kingdom for Christians – *The Lord will…bring me safely to His Heavenly Kingdom* (2 Tim. 4:18).

> *The church of the firstborn,* **whose names are written in Heaven**…*the spirits of righteous men made perfect* (Hebrews 12:23).

Finally, there will be the fulfilment of God's purposes when there will be – *A new Heaven and a new earth* (Rev. 21:1); *Amen. Come, Lord Jesus* (Rev. 22:20).

CHAPTER EIGHTEEN

PRAYER – SEEKING GOD'S KINGDOM

*Jesus said, "**When you pray, do not keep on babbling** like pagans, for they think they will be heard because of their many words. **Do not be like them, for your Father knows what you need before you ask Him**"* (Matthew 6:7-8).

Matthew chapter six records Jesus' instructions concerning prayer. It can be seen from this passage, and other Scriptures, that prayer is not meant to be centred upon our life and needs.

'Watch your motive before God; have no other motive in prayer than to know Him' (Oswald Chambers).

What is known as the Lord's Prayer (Matt. 6:9-13), begins with praise and a desire that God's Kingdom is established – *Our Father in Heaven,* **hallowed be your name, your Kingdom come***, your will be done on earth as it is in Heaven.* Jesus continued, by warning them against becoming self-absorbed in their requests – take their eyes off themselves and stop worrying.

*"Do not worry, saying, 'What shall we eat?' or 'What shall we drink?' or 'What shall we wear?' For the pagans run after all these things, and your Heavenly Father knows that you need them. **But seek first His Kingdom and His righteousness**, and all these things will be given to you as well"* (Matthew 6:31-33).

'The purpose of prayer is not to inform God of our needs, but to invite Him to rule our lives' (Clarence Bauman).

We are meant to communicate with the Spirit throughout the day, as He leads and guides us. He will help us in all aspects of life. But let us resist becoming self-centred about our needs. Paul gives us insight into prayer in his letters to the churches.

PRAYER FOR THE EPHESIAN CHURCH

I have not stopped giving thanks for you, *remembering you in my prayers. I keep asking that the God of our Lord Jesus Christ, the glorious Father, may give you the Spirit of **wisdom and revelation, so that you may know Him better**. I pray also that **the eyes of your heart may be enlightened** in order that you may know the hope to which He called you, **the riches of His glorious inheritance in the saints**, and His incomparable great power for us who believe*
(Ephesians 1:16-19).

It is noticeable that Paul's prayer did not mention any needs. It focuses upon the Lord, and His work in their lives. He begins with thankfulness – *I have not stopped giving thanks for you.*

Sing and make music in your heart to the Lord, **always giving thanks** *to God the Father for everything, in the name of our Lord Jesus Christ* (Ephesians 5:19-20).

Paul prayed that they would have *the Spirit of **wisdom** and **revelation***. The Spirit imparts wisdom – *The Holy Spirit will teach you all things* (John 14:26). He will give revelation of the Lord – *He will bring glory to me* (John 16:14). The reason for doing this is – *so that they may know Him (Christ) better* (v. 17).

He prayed that – *the eyes of their heart be enlightened to our hope (in Christ)* (v. 18). He centred their attention upon the Lord – *In His great mercy God has given us new birth into a **living hope** through the resurrection of Jesus Christ* (1 Peter 1:3).

Paul then prays that they will truly understand what takes place in us when we are born again – we receive a *glorious inheritance* (v. 18), together with God's *incomparable great power* (v. 19). These are the things that Paul focussed upon, and what he also wanted the church to meditate and reflect upon.

PRAYER FOR THE PHILIPPIAN CHURCH

I thank my God every time I remember you. In all my prayers for all of you, **I always pray with joy because of your partnership** *in the gospel...And this is my prayer: that your love may* **abound more and more in knowledge and depth of insight**, *so that you may* **be able to discern what is best and may be pure and holy** *until the day of Christ,* **filled with the fruit of righteousness** *that comes through Jesus Christ – to the glory and praise of God* (Philippians 1:3-11).

Paul began by giving thanks. He expressed the *joy* (v. 4) he encountered through being in *partnership* (v. 5) with the church at Philippi. Although he was an Apostle, he did not get caught up in position or status. He regarded the people as partners.

His prayer was that they would *abound more and more in depth of insight* (v. 9). He sought that, like him, they would have more and more revelation into the mystery that God has revealed in Christ Jesus.

The mystery made known to me by revelation...In reading this, then, you will be able to understand my **insight into the mystery of Christ**, *which was not made known to men in other generations as it has now been revealed by the Spirit* (Ephesians 3:3-5).

He also prayed that they would *be able to discern what is best* (v. 10) – *The spiritual man makes judgements about all things* (1 Cor. 2:15). It is important that we discern that which is ungodly in order that we live a *pure* (v. 10) lifestyle.

The result of living in such a manner is that we will be – *filled with the fruit of righteousness* (v. 11). We live righteously in response to receiving Christ's righteousness within us (Rom. 8:10). We do so – *to the glory and praise of God* (v. 11).

PRAYER FOR THE COLOSSIAN CHURCH

*We always thank God when we pray for you...Since the day we heard about you, we have not stopped praying for you and asking God to **fill you with the knowledge of His will through all spiritual wisdom and understanding**. And we pray this in order that you may **live a life worthy of the Lord** and may please Him in every way: bearing fruit in every good work, **growing in the knowledge of God**, being **strengthened with all power** according to His glorious might so that you may have great endurance and patience, and joyfully giving thanks to the Father* (Colossians 1:3-12).

Once again, there is no mention of needs in Paul's prayer. It is all centred upon Christ, receiving revelation and living in response to Him – *joyfully giving thanks to the Father* (v. 12).

There is no point in constantly telling God about our needs as some are prone to do. Jesus said, **"Do not babble...Do not be like them, for your Father knows what you need before you ask Him"** (Matt. 6:7-8). We are obviously meant to ask the Holy Spirit to help us make judgements, and to know the best way of dealing with a situation. But when we ask Him for guidance, we do so in the knowledge that He already knows all about it.

'Though we cannot by our prayers give God any information, yet we must by our prayers give Him honour' (Matthew Henry).

Paul prayed that the Colossian Church would be *full of the knowledge of His will through all spiritual wisdom and understanding...in order that they live a life worthy of the Lord...grow in the knowledge of God, being strengthened with all power so that they would have great endurance and patience.*

These principles reveal the core of prayer.

CHAPTER NINETEEN

PRAYER - LISTENING

Be joyful always; **pray continually**; *give thanks in all circumstances, for this is God's will for you in Christ Jesus* (1 Thessalonians 5:16-18).

During the course of each day, either in work or at home, certain duties require that we fully concentrate on the respective task in which we are engaged, whether it is mental or physical. When that duty is complete, and we no longer need to fully focus our concentration, what do we then think about? What occupies our thoughts throughout the majority of the day?

*Since, then, you have been raised with Christ, set your hearts on things above...**Set your minds on things above**, not on earthly things* (Colossians 3:1-2).

In the above verse (1 Thess. 5:16), Paul encouraged the believers to *pray continually*. He wanted them to understand, and experience, continual communion with the Lord.

Jesus was fully divine and fully human. He subjected Himself to humanity, and revealed to His disciples how to daily be in relationship with the Father; one aspect of which is prayer.

One day Jesus was praying in a certain place. *When He finished, one of His disciples said to Him,* **"Lord, teach us to pray**, *just as John taught his disciples"* (Luke 11:1).

The disciple saw that Jesus prayed differently, and he wanted to be like Him. What happened in those times of prayer that Jesus had with the Father? – *Everything I* **learned** *from my Father I have made known to you* (John 15:15): *My food is to* **do the will of Him** *who sent me* (John 4:34). In order to *learn* and to *do the will of God*, Jesus **continually** communed with the Father.

THE PLACE OF LISTENING

Offer your bodies as living sacrifices, *holy and pleasing to God – this is your spiritual act of worship. Do not conform any longer to the pattern of this world, but be transformed by **the renewing of your mind**. Then you will be able to test and approve **what God's will is*** (Romans 12:1-2).

The Old Testament Temple was made up of three parts: the outer and inner courts where sacrifices took place, and the priests washed themselves; the Holy Place where the priests ministered to God; the Holy of Holies in which God's presence resided, and from where He spoke to the High Priest. There are direct parallels between the Old Testament Temple, and how we function as *the temple of the Holy Spirit* (1 Cor. 3:16; 6:19) under the New Covenant (Heb. 8:6) that Jesus established.

Just like the Temple, we also comprise of three parts – *spirit, soul and body* (1 Thess. 5:23). Our body represents the outer courts, that which is visible; our soul is the Holy Place where we minister to God by changing into His image; our spirit is the Holy of Holies where Christ's presence resides by His Spirit.

Romans 12:1-2 teaches how to *renew our mind*. But it also reveals how we enter that place with the Lord, where we are still in His presence, listening to His voice. We are encouraged to *offer our bodies as living sacrifices*. We enter the **outer courts** where we offer the sacrifice of time; in our bodies we physically set aside time for the Lord, bringing our *sacrifice of praise* (Heb. 13:15). We then enter the **Holy Place** where we worship the Lord by stilling our soul; *we do not conform to the pattern of the world* which seeks its own glory, and what they can get for themselves. Instead, we renew our mind to – *Be still and know that I am God* (Psalm 46:10). We are then ready to enter the **Holy of Holies** (Most Holy Place), into His presence. It is the place where He speaks to us in our spirit, to know *His will*.

SPIRITUAL TRUTHS IN SPIRITUAL WORDS

We speak, *not in words taught us by human wisdom but in words taught by the Spirit,* ***expressing spiritual truths in spiritual words*** (1 Corinthians 2:13).

We continually carry the presence of God within us because the Lord Jesus resides within our spirit by the Holy Spirit. But there are also moments when we enter His presence by stilling ourselves. Some of these times we just spend in worship; other times we are just quiet; and sometimes we listen to Him as He guides us through His Word, or directs us by His Spirit; we learn to hear His will as we saw in the beginning of the chapter. The more we practise the presence of the Lord, the more we will recognise His voice, as we shall see later in chapter twenty-four.

Most of our earthly conversation is quickly forgotten. It is general talk and just part of enjoying one another's company, as we share humour, take an interest in other peoples' lives, or discuss topics. But, sometimes, something is said that is very significant, that is remembered, and impacts a person's life.

When we practise *being still, and knowing that He is God* (Psalm 46:10), we hear *spiritual truths in spiritual words* (1 Cor. 2:13). He speaks to us through His Word and Spirit. The more we develop that listening ear, alone in His presence, the more sensitive we become to His voice in the company of others. We discover that we impart wisdom in a difficult situation, or we have a verse of Scripture, or a word of encouragement for someone, which is unplanned and suddenly comes from within us. It is the Lord speaking to us from our spirit.

Every Christian can experience these things. We learn *spiritual truth and words* by entering His presence without any agenda; we do not seek anything for ourselves; we do not have a list of requests. We just want to *know Him better* (Eph. 1:17).

DECLARING WHAT WE HAVE HEARD

I have put my words in your mouth**. See, today I appoint you over nations and kingdoms to **uproot and tear down**, to **destroy and overthrow**, to **build and to plant (Jeremiah 1:9-10).

A born-again believer has great authority in and through the Lord Jesus – *He anointed us...You have an anointing from the Holy One...The anointing you received from Him remains in you* (2 Cor. 1:21; 1 John 2:20 & 27).

In the above verses, God revealed to Jeremiah that when he spoke the words that God gave him he would *uproot and tear down, destroy and overthrow, and build and plant*. Jesus said, *"The words I have spoken to you are spirit and they are life"* (John 6:63). The words that Jesus spoke into situations had a dramatic effect upon those that encountered them. His *anointing* is within us in order to do the same. As we saw earlier, we are able to *speak spiritual truths in spiritual words* (1 Cor. 2:13).

*Jesus said, "I tell you the truth, **if you have faith and do not doubt...you can say** to this mountain, 'Go, throw yourself into the sea,' and it will be done. **If you believe, you will receive what you ask for in prayer**"* (Matthew 21:21-22).

Jesus linked what we ask for in prayer, with speaking into a situation. As we have already seen from Scripture - ***Your Father knows what you need before you ask Him***" (Matt. 6:7-8). We go to Him, asking for guidance, not endlessly going over issues that He already knows. Having received direction from His Word and His Spirit, He wants us to exercise faith by declaring what He tells us – *If you have faith and do not doubt, **you can say***. He wants us to declare the *spiritual truths in spiritual words* that we hear in His presence. In His authority, we *speak to the mountain*. Prayer mixed with declaration is powerful.

CHAPTER TWENTY

PRAYER – WATCH AND PRAY

Devote yourselves to prayer, being watchful and thankful (Colossians 4:2).

Paul concludes his letter to the Colossian Church with an encouragement to *devote yourselves to prayer*; at the same time revealing key elements in prayer – **being watchful and thankful**.

The prophet Isaiah recorded the way in which we keep *watch – Let him be alert, fully alert* (Isaiah 21:6-7). The lookout responded – *Day after day, my Lord, I stand on the watchtower; every night I stay at my post* (Isaiah 21:8). He remained focussed on watching and waiting. Prayer involves self-discipline.

Habakkuk knew these principles. He wanted to *see and hear – **I will stand at my watch** and station myself on the ramparts; **I will look to see what He will say to me*** (Hab. 2:1).

Jesus asked His disciples to stand with Him in prayer. He wanted them to *watch and pray*; to remain focussed; to support Him. Unfortunately, they fell asleep.

*"Could you men not keep watch with me for one hour?" He asked Peter. "**Watch and pray** so that you will not fall into temptation. The spirit is willing, but the body is weak"* (Matthew 26:40-41).

The greatest thing we can give God is our time, because that act reveals our love, worship and service. We willingly *stay at our post* (Isaiah 21:8). At the same time as keeping watch, we *guard our heart* (Prov. 4:23) by remaining *thankful* (Col. 4:2).

***Always giving thanks to God the Father for everything**, in the name of our Lord Jesus Christ* (Ephesians 5:20).

PRAYER SUPPORT

And pray for us, too, *that God may open a door for our message, so that we may proclaim the mystery of Christ, for which I am in chains. Pray that I may proclaim it clearly, as I should* (Colossians 4:3-4).

In addition to encouraging them to be *watchful and thankful* (Col. 4:2), Paul also asked them to support him and his companions in prayer, in order that *a door is opened for their message*. He wanted them to know that they were joined with him, as he was with them; because all believers are one in the Spirit, in the Body of Christ. We stand with one another.

The body is a unit, though it is made up of many parts; and though all its parts are many, they form one body. So it is with Christ. ***For we were all baptised by one Spirit into one body*** (1 Corinthians 12:12-13).

Paul asked for their support in prayer, believing that they would respond to his request. He taught the importance of knowing that we are all *partners* in the Gospel, as he revealed to the Philippian Church.

*In all my prayers for all of you, I always pray with joy because of **your partnership in the Gospel** from the first day until now, being confident of this, that He who began a good work in you will carry it on to completion* (Philippians 1:4-6)

Ephesians 6:18 encourages us to *pray in the Spirit*. When we are sensitive to the leading and guiding of the Spirit, we will ***be alert*** to His promptings, when to uphold someone in prayer.

Pray in the Spirit *on all occasions with all kinds of prayers and requests. With this in mind,* ***be alert and always keep on praying for all the saints*** (Ephesians 6:18).

PRAYER FOR UNBELIEVERS

*Now to Him who is able to establish you by my gospel and the proclamation of Jesus Christ...**so that all nations might believe and obey Him*** (Romans 16:25-26).

Our Heavenly Father's will is *that all nations might believe and obey Him*. It occurs by – *the proclamation of Jesus Christ*.

Nowhere in Scripture does it state that we are to pray for God to save an individual, or a people – that they become born again. The reason that there is no need to pray to Him in such a way is that He has already stated in His Word that it is His will that everyone should receive His salvation through Christ Jesus.

1. *Jesus said, "For **my Father's will is that everyone** who looks to the Son and believes in Him shall have eternal life, and I will raise him up at the last day"* (John 6:40).
2. **God wants all men to be saved** *and to come to a knowledge of the truth* (1 Timothy 2:3-4).
3. *The Lord is patient with you,* **not wanting anyone to perish***, but everyone to come to repentance* (2 Peter 3:9).

We do not have to keep asking God to save people, when He has already declared to us in His Word that it is His will. His desire for that to happen is clear (John 3:16). Jesus explained to His disciples what we are to ask for in prayer concerning people being saved – *The harvest is plentiful, but the workers are few.* ***Ask the Lord of the harvest, therefore, to send out workers into His harvest field.*** *Go! I am sending you* (Luke 10:2-3).

Faith comes by hearing, and hearing by the Word of God (Rom. 10:17). That being the case, the Lord wants us to pray that His Word is taken to all people. As well as praying for someone, we speak His Word into their life, or ask in prayer that a fellow **worker** in the Lord speaks to them, so that their eyes are opened.

MAKING REQUESTS

Give us today our daily bread (Matthew 6:11).

There is a time in prayer to make requests; we are to *cast our cares upon the Lord* (Psalm 55:22; 1 Peter 5:7). But as we have seen in the previous chapters, they are a minor part. Our prayer life is not meant to be centred upon ourselves.

Jesus told us to ask for our daily sustenance – *our daily bread*. This has a wide significance; it is far more than just a list of personal requests. It is centring our focus upon the Lord, and understanding that He Himself is our daily bread – *Jesus declared, "I am the bread of life. He who comes to me will never go hungry, and he who believes in me will never be thirsty"* (John 6:35).

When we make requests to the Lord, we go in the knowledge and confidence that He knows and provides everything that we need; not necessarily what we want. We are to simply trust Him – *The Lord is my Shepherd,* ***I lack nothing*** (Psalm 23:1).

Sometimes, we do not see victory because we do not 'speak into' the situation that we face; we have not acted in faith by standing upon what His Word declares – *If you have faith...****you can say*** (Matt. 17:20). This, of course, does not mean that we can declare anything. It has to be according to God's will; in line with His Word; we cannot just focus upon our own 'wish list.'

We ask Him for direction from His Word and Spirit, and then declare it in faith for as long as it takes; not giving up.

*This is the confidence we have in approaching God: that **if we ask anything according to His will, He hears us**. And if we know He hears us – whatever we ask – we know that we have what we asked of Him* (1 John 5:14-15).

CHAPTER TWENTY-ONE

KNOW HIM BETTER

I keep asking that the God of our Lord Jesus Christ, the glorious Father, may give you the Spirit of wisdom and revelation, **so that you may know Him better** (Ephesians 1:17).

The Apostle Paul wrote the above words to the church at Ephesus. They were already **believers**; they were in relationship with the Lord Jesus. But Paul's desire was that that they would *know Him (Christ Jesus) better*.

When we first meet our future wife or husband, we can form a picture of what we believe them to be. We can be attracted to them; they can have many good qualities, together with an engaging personality. But in order for it to develop into a meaningful relationship we need to really get to know them. We do so by spending as much time as possible in their company.

Believing something about someone is the first step. Getting to **know** them is the part where we grow and bond together.

This second stage in our relationship with the Lord Jesus, whereby we get to *know Him better*, is the part where we enter a greater understanding of discipleship. We begin to hold onto His Word more consistently, and discover how it impacts our life. Believing the truth of Scripture is vital. But *knowing*, and applying it, is taking a step further in our walk with the Lord.

Jesus said, ***"If you hold to my teaching, you are really my disciples****. Then you will know the truth, and the truth will set you free"* (John 8:31-32).

We *believe* great things of the Lord. But let us also spend quantity and quality time with Him in order to really *know Him*.

FULLY KNOWN

I want to know Christ and the power of His resurrection and the fellowship of sharing in His sufferings, becoming like Him in His death (Philippians 3:10).

This statement by Paul reveals his motivation in life. In modern-day language – 'this is what got him out of bed in the morning.' The Lord was not a segment of his life, to which he periodically paid attention. Paul's fulfilment was in Him.

What prompts us to know someone better? Love is the answer.

I pray that you...grasp how wide and long and high and deep is the love of Christ, **and to know this love that surpasses knowledge** *– that you may be filled to the measure of all the fullness of God* (Ephesians 3:17-19).

Paul wanted to *grasp how wide and long and high and deep is the love of Christ*. It can be seen from all of Paul's letters that relationship with the Lord was the central factor in his life. He also knew that by experiencing that width, length, height and depth, he would become more like Christ Jesus. The more time we spend with someone, the more we are influenced by them.

And we, who with unveiled faces all reflect the Lord's glory, are **being transformed into His likeness** *with ever-increasing glory, which comes from the Lord, who is the Spirit* (2 Corinthians 3:18).

In eternity we will come into full revelation and relationship with the Lord. But He also gives us insight in the present time.

Now I know in part*; then I shall know fully, even as I am fully known* (1 Corinthians 13:12).

NOTHING ELSE COMPARES

I consider everything a loss **compared to the surpassing greatness of knowing Christ Jesus my Lord**, *for whose sake I have lost all things. I consider them rubbish that I might gain Christ* (Philippians 3:8).

In earlier days, Paul had been a very religious individual. He was focussed on achieving 'godliness' through his own self-drive and *legalistic righteousness*.

If anyone else thinks he has reason to put confidence in the flesh, I have more: ...in regard to the Law, a Pharisee; as for zeal, persecuting the church; as for **legalistic righteousness**, *faultless* (Philippians 3:4-6).

After encountering the Lord Jesus on the road to Damascus (Acts 9:1-5), Paul had a different understanding of *knowing* God. He came to realise that it is by relationship, not religious tradition and behaviour that we come to know our Heavenly Father. This can only be obtained through Christ Jesus.

Be found in Him (Christ), not having a righteousness of my own *that comes from the Law, but that which is* **through faith in Christ** – *the righteousness that comes from God and is by faith* (Philippians 3:9).

Paul stated that *for the sake of* **knowing Christ Jesus** he had *lost all things* (Phil. 3:8). Among those things that he lost was his self-righteousness, and religiosity. He was prepared to lay down his ambition, status in the community, and position.

Like Paul, we discover that the things to which we formerly attached importance, no longer have the same value. We do not even have to consciously give them up. They simply drop away, because of the **surpassing greatness of knowing Christ Jesus**.

ALL OF HIM

*I want to know Christ and the **power of His resurrection** and the fellowship of **sharing in His sufferings**, becoming like Him in His death* (Philippians 3:10).

In Chapter Ten we saw that the Lord Jesus is referred to as the *Lion* (Rev. 5:5) and the *Lamb of God* (John 1:29; 1 Peter 1:19). The characteristics of a lion are its majesty and strength, indicating royalty and rule. Reference to a lamb reveals a submissive attitude, a lowly position; the nature and character of Christ's sacrifice. The Lord encompasses both authority and humility. Jesus gave us the pattern of how we also are to live – with authority, but accompanied by a humble attitude.

In the above verse (Phil. 3:10), Paul describes that *knowing Christ* means embracing each of the above principles; of authority (*the power of His resurrection*); and humility (*sharing in His sufferings, becoming like Him in His death*).

We are not meant to 'pick and choose' what we want to experience in our relationship with the Lord. Paul revealed that he wanted to *know* all of Christ. He wanted to see the Kingdom of God revealed by using the authority of the Lord Jesus; but also to remain humble in attitude, so that *His will be done* (Matt. 6:10). Paul recognised that authority and humility cannot be separated if we are really serious about *knowing Christ*.

The same can be seen in the *gifts of the Spirit* (1 Cor. 12:4-11), and the *fruit on the Spirit* (Gal. 5:22-23). The *gifts* empower us; the *fruit* matures us. In the same manner as authority and humility, we are not to concentrate on one aspect at the expense of another. It is to embrace all of Him.

*He made known to us the mystery of His will...**which He purposed in Christ*** (Ephesians 1:9).

CHAPTER TWENTY-TWO

KNOWING OURSELVES BETTER

I praise you because I am fearfully and wonderfully made (Psalm 139:14).

We are a wonderful creation. Our spirit is that part of us where the Lord resides within us by the Holy Spirit. Our body is capable of incredible feats, and has the ability to survive extreme pressures; our soul is equipped with faculties that enable us to discover and cope with a wide diversity of experiences.

When we are born again, the Lord Jesus enters our spirit by the Holy Spirit, who then *seals* it (Eph. 1:13). The devil has no access to that part of us whatsoever.

Our soul is the 'battleground.' Our spirit is completely renewed at our salvation; whereas our soul enters a process of restoration. It is through the Word of God, and the teaching, leading and guiding of the Holy Spirit that change occurs. There are no short cuts to the restoration of our soul. It is dependent upon our willingness to be *transformed* (Rom. 12:1-2).

When we apply His Word to our life we learn the principles of capturing our thoughts, and renewing our **mind**. Our **heart** is then full of good things that create the values that our **conscience** operates from. Our **emotions** become harnessed and under control, so that our **will** can make clear decisions. We develop strength of **character**; our **temperament** becomes well-balanced; all of these interact with one another to display a positive and attractive **personality**.

In this second part of the book where we examine *knowing Him better* (Eph. 1:17), it is also important that we understand how the different parts of our soul interact. By doing so, we will discover how His Word and Spirit can change us for the better.

MIND – HEART – EMOTIONS

Our **mind** is the doorway to our soul. What we dwell upon each day has an effect upon the other parts of our soul. 'If we are not responsible for the thoughts that pass our doors, we are at least responsible for those we admit and entertain' (Charles Newcomb). Thoughts that are fleeting, or of medium duration do not generally have any lasting effect. But those that we continually churn over in our mind will have a consequence, either for the good or for the bad. That is why the Word of God instructs us to practise *capturing our thoughts* (2 Cor. 10:5), and to be – *transformed by* **the renewing our mind** (Rom. 12:1-2).

Thoughts that we dwell upon, subsequently pass through the 'door' of our mind, and produce the content of our **heart**. It is the place where our attitudes and opinions are formed. That is why Scripture warns us – *Above all else,* **guard your heart***, for it is the wellspring of life* (Prov. 4:23). Our words have their root in the attitudes of our heart. Jesus explained that our heart is like a storehouse – *Out of the overflow of the heart the mouth speaks* (Matt. 12:34). What comes out of our mouth will come from what is stored within our heart, whether it is good or bad.

The content of our mind and heart affect our **emotions**. If we do not *renew our mind* and *guard our heart*, then we will be unable to control our emotions. At creation, God gave us emotions so that we can have pleasure, be compassionate etc. But they are meant to inspire us; not rule us. If our emotions are not harnessed properly they will get out of control, and produce a negative effect upon ourselves, and others. Self-control is part of the *fruit of the Spirit* (Gal. 5:22). Therefore, every born-again believer has the capacity to be in control of their emotions. The Word encourages us – *Prepare your minds for action;* **be self-controlled** (1 Peter 1:13). If we have developed a pattern of negative emotions, then we can change by training ourselves to capture our thoughts, becoming sensitive to the Spirit within us.

CONSCIENCE – WILL

Our **conscience** operates according to the values that we have adopted; but it does not govern what we believe. It reacts to the principles that we have embraced, and already believe. Our conscience is governed by what we dwell on in our mind, and subsequently store in our heart. That is why our conscience can react in a different manner to that of other people. One person may view something as being unacceptable, while another person considers it appropriate to continue.

When we are born again, our conscience is shaped by a new set of values and principles, namely the Word of God. Our thoughts become transformed by the *renewing of our mind* (Rom. 12:1-2); our *heart is set on things above* (Col. 3:1). This changes our approach to all aspects of our daily lifestyle. Consequently, this has a dramatic affect upon our conscience. Paul declared – **My conscience confirms it in the Holy Spirit** (Rom. 9:1). When considering matters, Paul listened to that 'inner voice' within him – *the mind of Christ* (1 Cor. 2:16), who is the Holy Spirit within our spirit.

Our **will** is the mental faculty by which we deliberately choose or decide upon a course of action. Everybody has some degree of willpower, which is the ability to exert control over conflicting mental and emotional issues. Our willpower develops strength according to the amount of time and energy we apply to it. It can be compared to physical exercise. Unpractised muscles produce an unhealthy body. Likewise, a will that does not develop decisiveness becomes weak, and prone to indecision and uncertainty. This leads to lack of confidence and motivation.

The evidence of the new nature in a believer's life is that we are willing and eager to continually apply God's will (John 4:34; 1 Peter 5:2). It is not a hardship or a burden; it is our desire – **Your will be done on earth as it is in Heaven** (Matt. 6:10).

TEMPERAMENT – CHARACTER – PERSONALITY

Our **temperament** is the manner of thinking, behaving, or reacting that is distinctive of each individual. We are born with our temperament. There are four main types: **choleric** – strong willed, self-driven, desires to lead and independent minded; **sanguine** – enthusiastic and emotional, very much a people's person, who likes being in the centre of everything that is happening; **melancholic** – analyses a great deal, seeks perfection, sets high standards for themselves and others, but is also caring and thoughtful; **phlegmatic** – amiable, easygoing, seeks to avoid responsibility and confrontation.

We all display aspects of each type of temperament at different times. But, month by month, we are generally dominant in one. An awareness of our particular temperament will enable us to understand why we think or behave in a particular manner.

Our **character** is the combination of qualities or features that distinguishes one person from another; the moral or ethical nature of a person. It is built upon the values and convictions that we embrace. Our conscience will function according to the nature of our character; there will of course be certain differences in how such matters are outworked. When we are born again, our character is influenced by the nature and character of God, as revealed in His Word. We learn to live according to the *new self*, not the *old self* (Eph. 4:22-24).

Our **personality** is the outward expression of ourselves; the distinctive traits of mind and behaviour. Our mind, heart, emotions, conscience, will, temperament and character interact within us. These are outwardly expressed in our personality. Scripture declares – *Surely you (God) desire truth in the inner parts* (Psalm 51:6). Our personality ought to be a true reflection of the other parts of our soul. We *put off falsehood and speak truthfully* (Eph. 4:25); we do not *put on a mask* (1 Thess. 2:5).

CHAPTER TWENTY-THREE

MOMENTS

*"When your children ask you, 'What do these stones mean?' tell them that the flow of the Jordan was cut off before the Ark of the Covenant of the Lord...**These stones are to be a memorial**"* (Joshua 4:6-7).

The Lord God instructed Joshua to choose one man from each of the twelve tribes. Each of them took a stone from the middle of the Jordan River, and later, they collectively placed the twelve stones at Gilgal as a *memorial* to what God had done.

His Word gives examples of 'moments;' of encounters with Him. His love and care is continually toward us; but there are specific times that become woven into the fabric of our memory. He wants those times to not only be remembered by those involved, but also to stand as a testimony to others. This does not mean that we dwell on the past at the expense of the present.

'We do not remember days, we remember moments' (Cesare Pavese).
'We do not know the true value of our moments until they have undergone the test of memory' (Georges Duhamel).

Our lives consist of a series of 'moments.' Many of them simply drift away because we do not regard them as important; others become etched in our memory, because we periodically remember them. They are the ones that form the content of our memory. The question that each of us has to face is – What sort of moments am I creating that will fill my memory?

'I would be a very happy person if it wasn't for my memories' (Millner). This was said light-heartedly. But it also reveals a truth. Our memory re-visits those things that have been placed there. What are the **'moments'** that we are filling it with?

PREPARE FOR MOMENTS

Joshua told the people, **"Consecrate yourselves***, for tomorrow the Lord will do amazing things among you" ...The priests carrying the Ark of the Covenant went ahead of the people...As soon as the priests who carried the Ark reached the Jordan and their feet touched the water's edge, the water from upstream stopped flowing. It piled up in a heap a great distance away* (Joshua 3:5-16).

Is there anything that we can do to prepare for 'moments' with the Lord? The above verses give some of the principles.

Firstly, it starts with having the right attitude in our mind and heart. What do we truly desire? **Consecration and sanctification** mean – 'set apart to God.' We respond to Him by – *seeking first His Kingdom and His righteousness* (Matt. 6:33).

Secondly, God showed the necessity of **His Presence**, as revealed in the Ark of the Covenant, not only being with them, but also going before them. We still ourselves, to wait on Him.

Thirdly, the priests and the people acted in **obedience** to what God had told them. They were obedient to His words.

Fourthly, they remained **steadfast in faith**. The water stopped flowing *from upstream*. Therefore, when the priests placed their feet in the Jordan, the water continued flowing in front of them. The miracle occurred *as soon as the priests' feet touched the water's edge*, but it was upstream where it occurred. They could have been tempted to think – 'nothing is going to happen.' But they did not rely on their natural understanding.

God's love towards us is unconditional – we cannot earn it. But in order to hear from Him, and be used by Him, it requires that **we prepare ourselves**. We reveal to Him that we are ready.

MOMENTS WHEN THE LORD KNOCKS

I slept but my heart was awake. Listen! **My lover is knocking: "Open to me..."** (Song of Songs 5:2).

The Song of Songs is a prophetic message of the relationship between Christ (the lover) and His Church (the beloved).

The Lord encourages us to *ask, seek, and knock*. He gives us the promise – *Everyone who asks receives; he who seeks finds; and to him who knocks, the door will be opened* (Luke 11:9-10).

Not only do we seek fellowship with the Lord, but He also seeks to meet with us. He wants us to *knock* on His door; but He also *knocks* on ours saying, **"Open to me"** (Song of Songs 5:2).

The beloved had a heart for her lover – *I slept but my heart was awake* (Song of Songs 5:2). She was *still* (Psalm 46:10); there was no other interference. The 'moment' was right. Everything was ready for an encounter with Him. She heard her lover knocking, and was sure of His desire to meet with her.

Unfortunately, there was hesitation on her part – *I have taken off my robe; must I put it on again? I have washed my feet; must I soil them again?* (Song of Songs 5:3). Sadly, it then goes on to say – *I opened for my lover, but my lover had left; he was gone. My heart sank at his departure* (5:6). She had lost a 'moment' with Him because she turned her attention onto herself.

We can all learn from this Scripture. Firstly, we need to know that the Lord comes *knocking*, to have 'moments' with us. Secondly, we *open to Him*, irrespective of the circumstances. The beloved hesitated because she felt it was inconvenient at that particular time. We can all be guilty of knowing the prompting of the Spirit within us, but tell ourselves "I will spend time with Him later." Sadly, we can miss the 'moment.'

CREATE MOMENTS

Set your hearts and minds on things above*, not on earthly things* (Colossians 3:1-2).

There are 'moments' when the Lord has suddenly appeared to people, such as Moses (Ex. 3:1-10); Gideon (Judges 6:11-16); Paul (Acts 9:1-6). Today, there are numerous testimonies from around the world of the Lord suddenly appearing to people in visions and dreams, without them even having any previous knowledge of Him. By His Spirit He is *calling people into His Kingdom and glory* (1 Thess. 2:12); and also directing individuals to a specific work in His Kingdom (Acts 16:9-10).

There are 'moments' with the Lord that suddenly occur, seemingly without any prior indication. But the majority of moments with Him, where we get to *know Christ better* (Eph. 1:17), come from times when we prepare ourselves, as we saw earlier, together with **creating time for Him** – *Be still, and know that I am God* (Psalm 46:10). Being *still* is mental and physical.

He has promised – *Never will I leave you; never will I forsake you* (Heb. 13:5). By His Spirit, He is always within us (1 John 3:24). He speaks to us through His Word and Spirit.

There are also 'moments' when individually, and collectively, we encounter the Lord's Shekinah Glory – His tangible presence. It is as if His glory within us becomes so *ever-increasing* (2 Cor. 3:18) that it attracts and draws down the Shekinah Glory from Heaven. It is a taste of eternity with Him. These encounters with Him can last for minutes, hours or days.

Prior to such 'moments' there is usually an increased hunger and thirst for His Presence, coupled by a stillness and sense of awe. It is as if time stands still. Minds and hearts are consecrated – set apart to God. These moments are never forgotten.

CHAPTER TWENTY-FOUR

HEARING HIS VOICE – A LISTENING EAR

Jesus said, "He who has ears, let him hear"
(Matthew 11:15).

Not everyone hears our Heavenly Father, whether it be through His Word or the Holy Spirit. When Jesus spoke to the gathered crowds, He would often use the above phrase. It came after He told a parable, or explained a spiritual truth. He was saying to them, words to the effect, "This will be heard and understood by those who have a genuine desire to hear and know – those who have spiritual ears."

Jesus explained to His disciples that the words they heard from Him were not just ordinary words – *The words I have spoken to you are Spirit and they are life* (John 6:63). They were not to take these words for granted. They were to be treasured.

> **Blessed are your eyes because they see, and your ears because they hear**. *For I tell you the truth, many prophets and righteous men longed to see what you see but did not see it, and to hear what you hear but did not hear it*
> (Matthew 13:16-17).

Jesus told His disciples that after He physically left them, He would send the Counsellor (Holy Spirit) who would continue to teach His words to them – *When He, the Spirit of truth, comes, He will guide you into all truth* (John 16:13). We are able to understand spiritual truth through the Spirit, whom we receive in us when we are born again – *You know Him, for He lives with you and **will be in you*** (John 14:17).

> *We have not received the spirit of the world but **the Spirit who is from God, that we may understand what God has freely given us*** (1 Corinthians 2:12).

RE-TUNING OUR HEARING

Apply your heart *to instruction* ***and your ears*** *to words of knowledge* (Proverbs 23:12).

We receive the Holy Spirit within us after we are born again. We can come before the Lord twenty-four hours each and every day, and receive revelation and instruction from His Word and Spirit. We are also able to hear the Spirit as He leads and guides us in our daily lives.

However, this does not mean that, just because we are a Christian, we will automatically hear from God. In order to hear from Him we need to develop a 'spiritual ear.' Every day we are bombarded by voices. In order to discern that which is of the Spirit, it requires that we re-tune our hearing from the natural into the spiritual. This is a process that is practised and learned.

Prior to being born again we lived according to our five natural senses of sight, hearing, taste, touch and feel. After we become a Christian we receive the Holy Spirit, who gives us the ability to operate in a 'sixth sense' within us. We do not become proficient in hearing Him over-night; it has to be developed – *Train yourself to be Godly* (1 Tim. 4:7).

There is one thing that is essential in training ourselves to hear the Holy Spirit, namely – ***Be still, and know that I am God*** (Psalm 46:10). This is not easy in the fast pace of modern-day life; our mind can be juggling many different things. But if we are serious about having *ears to hear* (Matt. 11:15) it takes time; there are no short cuts. This does not mean that we have to wait for large amounts of time. It has more to do with our attitude of mind by learning to focus upon Him, even in busyness.

The mind controlled by the Spirit is life and peace (Romans 8:6).

COVERING EARS IN REBELLION

*They refused to pay attention; stubbornly they turned their backs and **stopped up their ears**. **They made their hearts as hard as flint** and would not listen to the law or to the words that the Lord Almighty had sent by His Spirit* (Zechariah 7:11-12).

The above verse reveals the consequence of *stopping up our ears* to God; it makes our *hearts as hard as flint*. His Word gives a very clear instruction about our spiritual heart – *Above all else, **guard your heart**, for it is the wellspring of life* (Prov. 4:23).

*Today, if you hear his voice, **do not harden your hearts**...See to it, that none of you has a sinful, unbelieving heart* (Hebrews 3:7-12; Psalm 95:7-8).

Hebrews was written to believers. It warns that, if our heart is hardened, we will not receive God's Word, which then leads to unbelief – *The message they heard was of no value to them, because those who heard did not combine it with faith* (Heb. 4:2)

One of the chief reasons for a hardened heart is that we cover our ears. The Lord, through His Word and His Spirit, could be telling us to do, or stop doing, something; but we do not want to listen at that point in time. It could be something as simple as apologising to someone, which we are reluctant to do. We *stop up our ears* for as long as possible. Unfortunately, it so often prevents us from hearing truth, because we do not *listen to the words that the Lord Almighty had sent by His Spirit*.

The link between what we hear, and that which enters our heart, is revealed in the words that God spoke to Ezekiel – ***Listen carefully and take to heart** all the words I speak to you* (Ezekiel 3:10). He had spiritual *ears* that were open to the words that God said to him. They entered his heart, and produced fruit.

COVERING OUR EARS IN FAITH

Avoid godless chatter, *because those who indulge in it will become more and more ungodly* (2 Timothy 2:16).

It is impossible to avoid negative and ungodly words; we are meant to engage with the world in order to reveal the love of God. But, as Paul points out, we are to be aware of senseless and negative conversation that is going nowhere. He later expanded upon the above instruction – *Don't have anything to do with foolish and stupid arguments, because you know they produce quarrels* (2 Tim. 2:23). Paul gave the same advice to Titus, which can also apply to conversation with other Christians.

Avoid foolish controversies *and genealogies and arguments and quarrels about the Law, because* ***they are unprofitable and useless*** (Titus 3:9).

The link between what we hear, dwell on, and then store in our heart, highlights the need to have *ears to hear* (Matt. 11:15) that which is good – *Faith comes by hearing, and hearing by the Word of God* (Rom. 10:17 King James Translation).

What we dwell on in our mind will become the content of our spiritual heart; the place where we form our attitudes and opinions. Our words proceed from that source – *Out of the overflow of the heart the mouth speaks* (Matt. 12:34).

Jesus said, *"He who has ears, let him hear"* (Matt. 11:15). This is a challenge to each of us. Do we have 'spiritual ears,' and what are they attuned to? It will be revealed in what we choose to hear and dwell on daily; whether it is in conversation, or that which we listen to and watch in the media.

O my people, hear my teaching; ***listen to the words of my mouth*** (Psalm 78:1).

CHAPTER TWENTY-FIVE

HEARING HIS VOICE - OBEDIENCE

The Lord is my shepherd; *I lack nothing* (Psalm 23:1).

In the Middle East, at the end of each day, the shepherds bring their individual flocks into one communal sheepfold where they are gathered together over-night, being protected by a gatekeeper. In the morning, the shepherds return and call their own sheep. Although the sheep are mixed together, each flock knows its own shepherd's voice. They leave the sheepfold, and follow him. They do not respond to anyone else.

May the God of peace, who through the blood of the eternal covenant brought back from the dead **our Lord Jesus, that great Shepherd of the sheep**, *equip you with everything good for doing His will* (Hebrews 13:20-21).

The shepherd leads his sheep out of the sheepfold, and they follow him to the ground where they graze during the morning. In the early afternoon he provides a temporary shelter built out of bushes and branches in which they are enclosed. They rest at that place, and are secure from attack by wild animals. The shepherd lies across the one opening to the enclosure. Access, both in and out, can only be gained via the shepherd.

I am the gate; *whoever enters through me will be saved. He will* **come in and go out, and find pasture**. *The thief comes only to steal and kill and destroy; I have come that they may have life, and have it to the full* (John 10:9-10).

Jesus revealed that He is the Shepherd that loves His sheep, even to the point of giving His life, so that they can live.

I am the good shepherd. *The good shepherd lays down His life for the sheep* (John 10:11).

RECOGNISE HIS VOICE

*When he has brought out all his own, he goes on ahead of them, and **his sheep follow him because they know his voice*** (John 10:4).

In order to recognise a voice we have to first of all *know* it. The sheep follow a shepherd because they are with him daily. They hear him over all others. How do we know the Lord's voice? It is through daily encountering His Word and Spirit.

If sheep were to accompany a shepherd just once in a while, they would not be able to recognise his voice when he calls. This would cause confusion. Likewise, if we do not spend time with the Lord, we will not recognise His voice when He speaks to us; we will be unable to discern those times when His Spirit leads and guides us.

The consequence of this is that we will be open to all manner of 'voices' who will lead us in all sorts of directions, which are not beneficial to our well-being. Jesus told His disciples to run from such voices.

*His sheep follow him because they know his voice. But they will never follow a stranger; in fact, **they will run away from him because they do not recognise a stranger's voice*** (John 10:4-5).

The thief comes only to steal and kill and destroy (John 10:10). The devil will use any means to direct us to a place where we become vulnerable. He speaks to us by implanting thoughts in our mind, or by using people who are susceptible to his ways. We are to be wise to his schemes.

...In order that Satan might not outwit us. For we are not unaware of his schemes (2 Corinthians 2:11).

LISTEN FOR HIS VOICE

The sheep listen to the shepherd's voice (John 10:3).

Listening is a skill that is learned. The temptation is to always be thinking of the next thing to say. We are given one mouth and two ears so that we listen twice as much as we speak. We get to know a person by listening. This principle is clearly seen in our relationship with the Lord.

'The first purpose of prayer is to know God' (Charles Allen).

'We look upon prayer as a means of getting things for ourselves. The Bible's idea of prayer is that we get to know God Himself' (Oswald Chambers).

Guard your steps when you go to the house of God. **Go near to listen** *rather than to offer the sacrifice of fools, who do not know that they do wrong. Do not be quick with your mouth; do not be hasty in your heart to utter anything before God* (Ecclesiastes 5:1-2).

One of the key elements of listening is expectancy. We listen, and pay attention, if we expect to hear something. We therefore need, first of all, to have the confidence that God truly wants to speak to every believer. **He calls us to listen to Him.**

Come*, all you who are thirsty, come to the waters; ...**Listen, listen to me**, and eat what is good, and your soul will delight in the richest of fare.* ***Give ear to and come to me; hear me****, that your soul may live* (Isaiah 55:1-3).

Jesus said, *"He who has ears, let him hear"* (Matt. 11:15). We saw in chapter twenty-four that, sadly, not everyone hears spiritually. The people who hear are those described in the above verse – those who *hunger and thirst;* they have attuned their *ear.*

OBEY HIS VOICE

I am the good shepherd; I know my sheep and my sheep know me (John 10:14).

Jesus is the good shepherd who loves us – *laying down his life for the sheep* (John 10:11). We respond to His love by obeying Him – *If anyone loves me, he will **obey my teaching*** (John 14:23).

Sheep obey the shepherd because they *know* and trust his voice; he will *find pasture* for them (John 10:9). If, each day, he calls them out of the sheepfold into a pack of wolves that attack them, or takes them to rocky ground where there is no pasture, they would become reluctant to follow him.

***The Lord is my shepherd**...He makes me **lie down in green pastures**, He leads me beside quiet waters* (Psalm 23:1-2).

In those times in life that are daunting and difficult, we can have faith, and no fear, because the *good shepherd* is always with us – *I will fear no evil, for you are with me* (Psalm 23:4).

Because He is *with us*, we can have confidence in the midst of opposition – *You prepare a table before me in the presence of my enemies* (Psalm 23:5). The table that He sets before us is full of all that we need to sustain us – *His divine power has given us **everything we need** for life and Godliness* (2 Peter 1:3).

Abraham *knew* and trusted God. Although he did not know the specific outcome of stepping out in faith, he *knew* that he could trust Him. Because of this, *by faith he obeyed Him.*

***By faith** Abraham, when called to go to a place he would later receive as his inheritance, **obeyed and went,** even though he did not know where he was going* (Hebrews 11:8).

CHAPTER TWENTY-SIX

INHERITANCE

I pray also that the eyes of your heart may be enlightened in order that you may know the hope to which He has called you, **the riches of His glorious inheritance in the saints** *and His incomparable great power for us who believe* (Ephesians 1:18-19).

When we are born again we come into a *glorious inheritance*. Its full significance will be encountered in eternity.

In God's great mercy He has given us new birth into a living hope through the resurrection of Jesus Christ from the dead, and into **an inheritance that can never perish, spoil or fade – kept in Heaven for you** (1 Peter 1:3-4).

There is not only a future inheritance awaiting us, but, also, our Father wants *the eyes of our heart enlightened* to the *glorious inheritance* that He places **in the saints** (Eph. 1:18-19) whilst still on earth. The inheritance that is deposited within us is Christ Jesus Himself, by the Holy Spirit.

God has chosen to make known among the Gentiles the glorious riches of this mystery, which is **Christ in you, the hope of glory** (Colossians 1:27).

The *riches* that we receive are not a small measure. We receive of Christ's fullness; such is God's grace and mercy towards us – *In Christ all the fullness of the Deity lives in bodily form, and* **you have been given fullness in Christ** (Col. 2:9-10).

The inheritance that we receive is **everything we need for life and Godliness** (2 Peter 1:3). He wants us to understand everything we have in Him, and that His 'resources' enable us to fulfil His individual plan and purpose for our life (Eph. 2:10).

UNCLAIMED INHERITANCE IN THE KINGDOM

*The country was brought under their control, but there were still seven Israelite tribes who **had not yet received their inheritance**. So Joshua said to the Israelites, "**How long will you wait before you begin to take possession of the land that the Lord, the God of your fathers, has given you?**"* (Joshua 18:1-3).

In the Old Testament, inheritance is mostly used in respect of land. In the New Covenant, it is our identity in Christ. However, the principles of coming into our inheritance run parallel. In the above verses, Joshua told the Israelites that God had already *given the land to them*.

He asked the seven tribes to whom it applied, *"How long will you wait before you receive your inheritance?"* In Christ, we receive *fullness* (Col. 2:9-10), and *everything we need* (2 Peter 1:3). Paul, under the leading of the Holy Spirit, says the same as Joshua, namely that we are to – *open the eyes of our heart to our inheritance* (Eph. 2:18-19). Our Father does not want us to be ignorant of what is already ours in Christ.

Joshua had previously told a tribe that wanted a larger inheritance – *Go up into the forest and clear land for yourselves* (Joshua 17:15). He told them that the inheritance was already there. All they had to do was make the effort of clearing land in order to make space. The same principle applies to us. We will only understand the inheritance we have in Christ when we take time to clear 'land' (space) inside us to discover more of Him.

Clearing the land involves examining those things in our life that take so much of our time and attention – *Be still, and know that I am God* (Psalm 46:10). This will result in us being more able to see our inheritance in Him, and in so doing, discover the plans and purposes that He has for each of us (Eph. 2:10).

THREE REASONS FOR UNCLAIMED INHERITANCE

1. Lack of knowledge – In the natural, there are people who remain poor, simply because they have no knowledge of an inheritance to which they are entitled. It is the same in the spiritual. A person can be born again, but not be fully aware of the *glorious riches in Christ* (Col. 1:27) that they have received. There is only one answer to this lack of knowledge, namely to meditate upon the Word of God (Rom. 10:17), and at the same time listen to the guidance of the Holy Spirit (John 16:13-15).

2. Lack of understanding – A person may have knowledge of the existence of an inheritance, but lacks the understanding that it is personally for them. A born-again believer can see other Christians rejoicing in their inheritance, but never seem to accept that it is for them as well. This is usually linked to a lack of knowledge of what the Word of God states concerning their identity in Christ. They may feel it is arrogant or presumptuous to claim such matters. But, Scripture instructs us to possess it.

*The (Holy) Spirit Himself testifies with our spirit that we are God's children. Now **if we are children, then we are heirs – heirs of God and co-heirs with Christ*** (Romans 8:16-17).

3. Lack of interest – The inheritance is already provided. The determining factor as to whether we come into its fullness will be desire. A person who does not have the desire will not have the motivation to claim what is rightfully theirs. But, if we do have that passion for the Lord, then we will seek to know all about Him through His Word, and by His Spirit. The writer to the Hebrews told the believers – *Solid food is for the mature, who **by constant use have trained themselves*** (Heb. 5:14). He gives some further teaching, which he followed by saying:

We want each of you to show the same diligence…*we do not want you to become lazy* (Hebrews 6:11-12).

EXPLORE OUR INHERITANCE IN THE KINGDOM

*Joshua said, "I will send them out to **make a survey** of the land and to write a description of it, **according to the inheritance of each**"* (Joshua 18:4).

As we saw earlier, there is an inheritance awaiting every born-again believer in Heaven (1 Peter 1:3-4). We will spend eternity with the Lord Jesus exploring its vastness. But, He also wants us to be an exploratory people whilst on earth – *Make a survey…according to the inheritance of each* (Joshua 18:4). We *make a survey*, and continually explore new territory through knowledge of God's Word – *Your Word is a lamp to my feet and a light for my path* (Psalm 119:105).

The questions we each need to ask ourselves are – What is the size of the ground that I am presently occupying? Am I living in the fullness of all that the Lord has for me? Are the *eyes of my heart enlightened to the glorious inheritance* that the Lord has given me? Figuratively speaking, am I willing to make the effort of exploring 'north, south, east and west' in His Kingdom?

*I pray that you…grasp how **wide** and **long** and **high** and **deep** is the love of Christ* (Ephesians 3:17-18).

When we are willing to set aside time each day to 'explore' the Lord Jesus, then we open ourselves up to continual revelation about Him through His Word and Spirit. In so doing, we discover more and more of our inheritance in Him. We also come to understand our individual inheritance – the plans and purposes that He has for each of us (Jer. 29:11).

*Lord, you have assigned me my portion and my cup; you have made my lot secure. **The boundary lines have fallen for me in pleasant places; surely I have a delightful inheritance*** (Psalm 16:5-6).

CHAPTER TWENTY-SEVEN

RENEWING OUR MIND – TRANSFORMED

Be transformed by the renewing of your mind
(Romans 12:2).

We comprise of *spirit, soul and body* (1 Thess. 5:23). Our spirit is that part of us that is born again – *Flesh gives birth to flesh, but **the (Holy) Spirit gives birth to (our) spirit*** (John 3:6).

Our soul consists of our mind, heart, emotions, will, conscience, temperament, character, and personality. Our spirit is instantly changed when we are born again because the Lord Jesus comes into that part of us by the Holy Spirit. From that moment in time our soul enters a process of transformation.

Jesus said, *"He who has ears, let him hear"* (Matt. 11:15). In order to develop a listening ear, our natural mind in our soul needs to be *renewed* according to the *mind of Christ* (1 Cor. 2:16) within our spirit. It starts when we are born again; it continues for the remainder of our life.

The *mind of Christ* is the Holy Spirit within our spirit. He teaches us the Word of God, together with guiding us in understanding God's will and purpose for our lives. The Spirit is within a born-again believer at all times.

*When He, the Spirit of truth, comes, **He will guide you into all truth**. He will not speak on His own; He will speak only what He hears, and He will tell you what is yet to come. He will bring glory to me by **taking from what is mine and making it known to you*** (John 16:13-14).

Jesus told His disciples – *The Holy Spirit will teach you all things* (John 14:26). Our response is to learn to still our natural mind in our soul, to listen to the *mind of Christ* in our spirit.

CAPTURING OUR THOUGHTS

*We demolish arguments and every pretension that sets itself up against the knowledge of God, and **we take captive every thought** to make it obedient to Christ* (2 Corinthians 10:5).

In order to *renew our mind* we have to learn how to *capture our thoughts*. If we fail to do so, we will continue to think in the old way instead of the new.

*Put off your old self...**to be made new in the attitudes of your minds**; and put on the new self* (Ephesians 4:22-24).

Our daily thought pattern generally fits into three categories: thoughts that are fleeting and inconsequential; those of a short or medium duration of time; thoughts that we hold onto and retain, because we dwell on them. It is the third category, those we dwell on and retain, that determine our state of mind.

If we dwell on something, whether it is positive or negative, we will have about five thoughts every thirty seconds. That can amount to fifty thoughts every five minutes. Test yourself.

Our mind is the entrance to our soul. All the other parts, namely our heart, emotions, will, conscience, temperament, character and personality are affected by what we think each day – *As a man thinks in his heart so he is* (Prov. 23:7 King James translation). Unless we develop in the fruit of the Spirit whereby we exercise *self-control* (Gal. 5:23) over our thoughts, we will not be able to effectively *renew our mind* (Rom. 12:1-2).

Although the Holy Spirit is within our spirit, and He will always seek to lead and guide in *all things*, it is noticeable that Scripture instructs us to *capture our thoughts* and to *renew our mind*. We have the responsibility in this particular area – *Prepare your minds for action;* ***be self-controlled*** (1 Peter 1:13).

IMPLEMENTING CHANGE

Since, then, you have been raised with Christ, **set your hearts** *on things above...**Set your minds** on things above, not on earthly things* (Colossians 3:1-2).

There are two types of capturing mentioned in the Bible.

The first involves capturing negative thoughts, in order to **protect** our soul (2 Cor. 10:5) – *Abstain from sinful desires,* **which war against your soul** (1 Peter 2:11).

The second is capturing and retaining positive thoughts in order to **restore** our soul (Psalm 23:3) – *Whatever is true, noble, right, pure, lovely, admirable – if anything is excellent or praiseworthy –* **think about such things** (Phil. 4:8).

By continually practising the first part, it enables us to apply the second, thereby *renewing our mind* (Rom. 12:1-2). Paul revealed that there are no short cuts – *Whatever you have learned or received from me* **put it into practice** (Phil. 4:9).

A professional sportsman practises day after day on the training ground. Because of his commitment and self-discipline he will automatically move into the correct position when the time comes for him to act. He does not even have to think before taking action. It has become instinctive.

When we daily train ourselves in capturing negative thoughts such as worry, doubt or unbelief we will discover that in a few months we will have changed almost without realising it.

Make every effort to add *to...knowledge, self-control; and to self-control, perseverance...If you possess these qualities in increasing measure, they will keep you from being ineffective* (2 Peter 1:5-8).

ENCOUNTERING CHANGE

We, who with unveiled faces all reflect the Lord's glory, **are being transformed into His likeness with ever-increasing glory**, *which comes from the Lord, who is the Spirit* (2 Corinthians 3:18).

When we are born again we have *peace with God* (Rom. 5:1). This is a finished act; it does not change. When we *renew our mind* we experience the *peace of God* affecting our daily life (Phil. 4:7). Peace with God is established; the peace of God is outworked. The more that our mind is *renewed* the greater will be the peace that *rules in our heart* (Col. 3:15). It does not come automatically; we have to apply God's peace to our life.

A *renewed mind* also produces a change in lifestyle. When we *know* the righteousness that has been imputed into us by Christ Jesus' Spirit, we respond to Him by living a holy life.

We know that when He appears, we shall be like Him, for we shall see Him as He is. **Everyone who has this hope in him purifies himself**, *just as He is pure* (1 John 3:2-3).

Another change that we encounter is greater love. When we dwell upon the love that we have received from God it creates a greater love for others – *We love because God first loved us* (1 John 4:19). A renewed mind learns to forgive – *Be kind and compassionate to one another, forgiving each other, just as in Christ, God forgave you* (Eph. 4:32).

These are just some of the changes that we encounter when we *renew our mind*. They develop as we mature in the Lord.

We will fail at times, but a *renewed mind* learns to quickly identify a sin or mistake, and not let it get worse. We then *press on* (Phil. 3:12) and continue to *be transformed into His likeness*.

CHAPTER TWENTY-EIGHT

RENEWING OUR MIND - PERSEVERING

It is in this middle stage of *knowing* that we truly enter discipleship. We cannot reach the level of maturity whereby we become *convinced* (2 Tim. 1:12) until we have experienced the discipleship of effectively applying His Word to our lives, and developing that listening *ear* (Matt. 11:15) to the Holy Spirit (John 16:13-15). We *renew our mind*. There are no short cuts.

It is good to pray for one another. It is also important to have 'spiritual fathers and mothers' to help disciple us in the Word of God. We are to *encourage one another* (Heb. 10:25). But there is also a path that we have to walk alone, where we do not rely on any other person, apart from the Lord Jesus, by His Spirit.

Discipleship begins when we are born again, and continues until we go to be with the Lord in eternity. He has plans and purposes for each one of us (Jer. 29:11) – *We are God's workmanship, created in Christ Jesus to do **good works, which God prepared in advance for us to do*** (Eph. 2:10). However, the reality of fulfilling those works will not happen unless we prove ourselves to be trustworthy – *Now it is required that those who have been given a trust **must prove faithful*** (1 Cor. 4:2).

> *We have much to say about this, but **it is hard to explain because you are slow to learn**. In fact, though by this time you ought to be teachers, **you need someone to teach you the elementary truths of God's Word all over again**. You need milk, not solid food!* (Hebrews 5:11-12).

The writer to the Hebrews was concerned about their lack of maturity in the Lord. He told the believers that they had not moved on in their application of the Word of God. They had not *proved faithful*. They had not grasped the basics of the faith; they were still 'spiritual babes.' It does not have to be that way.

TRAINING PROGRAMME

Train yourself to be Godly (1 Timothy 4:7).

The Apostle Paul was a 'spiritual father' to people like Timothy. He spent much time with him, discipling him in the Word and Holy Spirit. He imparted truth into many peoples' lives; but he knew that he could only do so much. They had to *train themselves to be Godly*. Paul knew that he could not *renew their minds* (Rom. 12:1-2); it is an individual responsibility.

The writer to the Hebrews, after confronting the churches about their lack of maturity, then explained to them the difference between being a believer and a disciple.

Solid food is for the mature, who **by constant use have trained themselves** (Hebrews 5:14).

From the context, it is clear that the letter was written to Christians; but they had remained in the basic *believing* stage. They had not taken responsibility to *train themselves*. The writer then goes on to encourage them to persevere in the things that he was teaching them, and how they could mature in the faith – *Show diligence…do not become lazy* (Heb. 6:11-12).

*Jesus said, "**If you hold to my teaching, you are really my disciples**. Then you will know the truth, and the truth will set you free"* (John 8:31-32).

The Lord made a clear distinction between a believer and a true disciple. There are many believers. But a disciple means – 'one who follows and actively applies His words;' they have *trained themselves* to *hold onto His teaching*. It does not get snatched away, die because of lack of depth, or get choked because of worries etc, as explained in the Parable of the Sower. Instead, the *seed* is held onto and produces a crop (Luke 8:1-15).

MAINTAINING OUR STAMINA

I do not run like a man running aimlessly; I do not fight like a man beating the air. No, ***I beat my body and make it my slave*** (1 Corinthians 9:26-27).

The words that Paul used are in the present tense. He was teaching them that *training to be Godly* (1 Tim. 4:7) is a continual process; it does not stop. In the above verse, he expressed his firm intention of remaining 'spiritually fit,' and that he would do whatever was necessary to maintain that fitness. He compares our spirituality with athletes who compete in the games; *they go into strict training* (1 Cor. 9:25).

One thing I do: forgetting what is behind and straining towards what is ahead, ***I press on*** *towards the goal to win the prize for which God has called me Heavenwards in Christ Jesus* (Philippians 3:13-14).

'Spiritual stamina' is similar to physical stamina; it is dependent upon our mental attitude. If our mind is not focussed, we will not effectively train, or prepare ourselves.

Any sportsman will verify that the race, fight, or match is won or lost in the mind. Likewise, as Christians, if we do not continually *renew our mind*, we will open the door to fear, doubt and worry; all of which will cause us to *run* at a slower pace.

Let us throw off everything that hinders *and the sin that so easily entangles, and* ***let us run with perseverance the race*** *marked out for us* (Hebrews 12:1).

Paul did not let his stamina diminish. His *mind was renewed* to the point where he was firmly focussed. Near the end of his life he was able to say – *I have fought the good fight,* ***I have finished the race****. I have kept the faith* (2 Tim. 4:7).

BUILDING UP OUR STRENGTH

Build yourselves up in your most holy faith *and pray in the Holy Spirit* (Jude 20).

How do we *build ourselves up* in our faith? How are we strengthened? – *Faith comes by hearing, and hearing by the Word of God* (Rom. 10:17 King James translation).

Strengthen me according to your Word (Psalm 119:28).

We reveal that we have been strengthened by His Word when we increasingly **hold to His teaching** (John 8:31). We keep a firm grip on His Word, not letting it slip through our fingers like sand. We become like a weightlifter, the more that our *hold* increases in strength, the more that we are able to lift and carry heavy weights. A firm grasp of Scripture will enable us to stand strong, even under considerable pressure.

The second part of Jude 20 instructs us to *pray in the Holy Spirit*. Speaking in tongues is a gift of the Spirit (1 Cor. 12:7-11). Paul continually spoke in tongues – *I thank God that I speak in tongues more than all of you* (1 Cor. 14:18). He encouraged its use – *Do not forbid speaking in tongues* (1 Cor. 14:39).

> *Anyone who speaks in a tongue does not speak to men but to God. Indeed, no-one understands him;* **he utters mysteries with his spirit…He who speaks in a tongue edifies himself** (1 Corinthians 14:2-4).

> ***I will pray with my spirit, but I will also pray with my mind;*** *I will sing with my spirit, but I will also sing with my mind* (1 Corinthians 14:15)

Being *built up in our most holy faith* is through the Word and the Spirit, developing a strong mind and faith.

CHAPTER TWENTY-NINE

RENEWING OUR MIND – SET FREE

*Jesus said, "**Remember the words I spoke to you**"* (John 15:20).

Part of the process of *renewing our mind* (Rom. 12:1-2) is remembering God's Word. We *hear* the Word (Rom. 10:17); *meditate* upon it (Joshua 1:8); *reflect* (2 Tim. 2:7); *hold onto* it (John 8:31); continually *remind* ourselves of the truth (2 Peter 1:12-13); take *action* in response to the truth (James 2:17).

The Galatian Church got into difficulty because they failed to *hold onto* God's Word. In consequence of this, they forgot *the words that had been spoken to them*. They no longer lived in the truth that they had originally received. The church was *thrown into confusion* by people who were propagating false doctrine.

I am astonished that you are so quickly deserting the one *who called you by the grace of Christ and are turning to a different gospel; which is really no gospel at all. Evidently,* **some people are throwing you into confusion** (Gal. 1:6-7).

The believers within the church failed to *capture* (2 Cor. 10:5) that which was ungodly. This occurred because they did not *hold onto* God's Word, which meant that they did not *know the truth*. Because of this, they were no longer *free* (John 8:32). They allowed themselves to be enslaved by false teaching.

It is for freedom that Christ has set us free. **Stand firm**, *then, and do not let yourselves be burdened again by a yoke of slavery* (Galatians 5:1).

Paul encouraged them to *stand firm*. We do so, by our mind being *renewed* according to the truth of God's Word. We learn to *stand* by *holding onto* the *words that He has spoken to us*.

TRUTH BRINGS FREEDOM

If the Son sets you free, you will be free indeed (John 8:36).

When we are born again, our spirit is made *alive because of (Christ's) righteousness* (Rom. 8:10). It is set free from sin and death – *The (Holy) Spirit gives birth to (our) spirit* (John 3:6). The devil has no access to our spirit because the Lord's presence continually resides there. It is therefore continually *free* from any ungodly influence. It is full of truth.

Our soul, which consists of our mind, heart, emotions, will, conscience, temperament, character and personality encounters freedom when it is renewed and restored according to the Word of God. If we do not learn to *renew our mind* (Rom. 12:1-2), by *holding onto His Word* (John 8:31), then we will not *know the truth*, and therefore we will not experience the *truth setting us free* (John 8:32). It is only through Christ that we are *set free*.

***Before this faith came, we were held prisoners by the law, locked up** until faith should be revealed* (Galatians 3:23).

In the above verse, Paul explained to the Galatian church that, prior to righteousness coming through Christ Jesus (Gal. 3:10-14), they were *held prisoners by the law, locked up*. They were held captive to a works and performance mentality; they did not know true freedom. He asked them – *Did you receive the (Holy) Spirit by observing the law, or by believing what you heard?* (Gal. 3:2); ***Do you wish to be enslaved all over again?*** (Gal. 4:9).

The *confusion* (Gal.1:7) in the Galatian Church was the direct result of them not *holding onto* God's Word. Their spirit remained *free* because of the Lord's presence in them by His Spirit; but those who were trying to live according to the Law had lost the freedom within their soul through confused thinking.

OUR MIND SET FREE

The mind controlled by the Spirit is life and peace
(Romans 8:6).

The world's perception of *control* is the opposite of *life and peace* (Rom. 8:6). They believe that control takes away your life and peace. But when we become a Christian, we discover a whole new way of thinking; the Spirit's control brings freedom.

When our mind is renewed according to God's Word, our understanding of things changes radically – ***Do not conform any longer to the pattern of this world****, but be transformed by the renewing of your mind* (Rom. 12:2). We realise that the submitting of ourselves to the Lordship of Christ brings us into a freedom that the world *cannot understand* (1 Cor. 2:14).

Paul asked the Galatian Church – *After beginning with the Spirit, are you now trying to attain your goal by human effort?* (Gal. 3:3). He was explaining to them that the Holy Spirit will only teach and guide us according to the Word of God. He told them that they were now in the New Covenant. Therefore, they were to stop trying to live the Christian life as if they were still under the old Covenant; which did not bring them into freedom.

Paul knew that if the Galatian Church were to forsake the work of the Spirit within them, they would resort to *trying by human effort*. They would lose *life and peace* (Rom. 8:6). Their mind would not know freedom; they would be *held prisoner* (Gal. 3:23) once more to guilt and condemnation. Being self-conscious of our 'performance' is the opposite of true freedom.

*I have been crucified with Christ **and I no longer live, but Christ lives in me**. The life I live in the body, I live by faith in the Son of God, who loved me and gave Himself for me* (Galatians 2:20).

VALUING OUR FREEDOM

You were called to be free. But do not use your freedom to indulge the flesh (Galatians 5:13).

The grace of God enables us to know that our sins are forgiven (2 Cor. 5:19). But His grace does not give us a licence to think or behave in an ungodly manner.

***The grace of God** that brings salvation has appeared to all men. **It teaches us to say "No" to ungodliness** and worldly passions, and to live self-controlled, upright and Godly lives* (Titus 2:11-12).

It is wonderful to be set free from the curse that resulted from not keeping all the rules and regulations pertaining to the Law – *Christ redeemed us from the curse of the Law by becoming a curse for us* (Gal. 3:13).

The Law was put in charge to lead us to Christ that we might be justified by faith. Now that faith has come, **we are no longer under the supervision of the Law** (Galatians 3:24-25)

But that does not mean that we can continue in sin.

What shall we say, then? **Shall we go on sinning, so that grace may increase? By no means!** *We died to sin; how can we live in it any longer?* (Romans 6:1-2).

The evidence of a *renewed mind* (Rom. 12:1-2) is that we know the freedom that we have through Christ, of not living subject to the Law. We are no longer held captive to guilt and condemnation. But, having received freedom, we respond to the Lord by highly valuing His grace, love and mercy that brings us that freedom. This causes us to focus our thoughts on that which is conducive to Godly living; we freely and willingly do so.

CHAPTER THIRTY

THE ANOINTING

God anointed us, set His seal of ownership on us, and put His Spirit in our hearts (2 Corinthians 1:21-22).

Anointed has the meaning of being declared sacred by God – set apart unto Him. When someone is born again, we change from being just a living being into a spiritual being (1 Cor. 15:44-49), because of Christ Jesus coming into our life by the Holy Spirit (1 John 3:24). The Anointing we receive from God *sets His seal of ownership on us* (2 Cor. 1:21).

The anointing oil used in the Old Testament was sacred. Exodus 30:22-33 describes the ingredients of how it was to be made, and then used to anoint the Tent of Meeting, and its contents, including the Ark of the Testimony. They were anointed to become consecrated and holy. There was an instruction that no other oil was to have the same formula; no other oil could be used as the Anointing oil (Ex. 30:32). It was sacred and unique; just like God's anointing upon a Christian.

The Anointing oil covered (spread over) the Tent of Meeting and its contents, which later became a fixed structure, namely The Temple. Both comprised of outer and inner courts, Holy Place and Most Holy Place. New Testament believers have become the *Temple of the Holy Spirit* (1 Cor. 3:16; 6:19).

We also comprise of three parts – *spirit, soul and body* (1 Thess. 5:23). In the same manner as the anointing oil covered the Tent of Meeting, so God's anointing covers us, *the Temple of the Holy Spirit*. We are His – *Sanctified in Christ Jesus and called to be holy* (1 Cor. 1:2). God makes us sacred and unique in Him.

You have an anointing from the Holy One…The anointing you received from Him remains in you (1 John 2:20; 27).

THE ANOINTED ONE

*The Spirit of the Sovereign Lord is on me, because **the Lord has anointed me*** (Isaiah 61:1).

The name 'Christ' literally means – 'The Anointed One.' When the Lord got up in the synagogue, as recorded in Luke 4:16-21, He quoted directly from Isaiah 61:1-2.

Jesus was both divine and human. He was anointed at the beginning of His earthly ministry:

*John (The Baptist) gave this testimony: "**I saw the Spirit come down from Heaven as a dove and remain on Him** (Jesus). I would not have known Him, except the One who sent me to baptise with water told me, 'The man on whom you see the Spirit come down and remain is He who will baptise with the Holy Spirit.' I have seen and I testify that this is the Son of God"* (John 1:32-34).

The Apostle Peter referred to the anointing upon Jesus:

God anointed Jesus of Nazareth with the Holy Spirit and power, *and He went around doing good and healing all who were under the power of the devil, because God was with Him* (Acts 10:38).

Isaiah prophesied of the effect of the Anointing coming upon Jesus – *Good news preached to the poor*; *broken-hearted bound*; *freedom for the captives*; *release for the prisoners*; *comfort for those who mourn*; *oil of gladness*; *become oaks of righteousness* (Isaiah 61:1-3). All that was fulfilled, and is still happening.

2 Corinthians 1:21 states – **God anointed us**. Jesus said, *"Anyone who has faith in me will do what I have been doing"* (John 14:12). God *anoints* us to do what Jesus did.

The Anointing

THE PURPOSE OF THE ANOINTING

I have found David my servant; ***with my sacred oil I have anointed him*** (Psalm 89:20).

In the Old Testament, whenever a Prophet, Priest or King entered service they were anointed, in order to receive God's blessing and equipping for their respective tasks. He gave the following instructions to Moses and Elijah:

Anoint *Aaron and his sons and consecrate them so they may serve me as* ***priests*** (Exodus 30:30).
Anoint *Jehu son of Nimshi* ***king*** *over Israel, and* ***anoint*** *Elisha to succeed you as* ***prophet*** (1 Kings 19:16).

As we have just seen, Jesus was *anointed* for service, and fulfilled each of the functions of Prophet, Priest and King:

Jesus of Nazareth was a ***Prophet*** (Luke 24:19).

We do have such a High ***Priest*** (Hebrews 8:1-2).

He is Lord of lords and ***King*** *of kings* (Revelation 17:14).

Just before Jesus ascended into Heaven, He commissioned His disciples to take His message into all the world. He told them that they would be empowered by the Holy Spirit (Acts 1:8). This occurred a few days later at Pentecost (Acts 2:1-4).

Those who encounter the Anointing (Isaiah 61:1-3) will – ***rebuild*** *the ancient ruins;* ***restore*** *the places long devastated;* ***renew*** *the ruined cities* (Isaiah 61:4). The Scripture then goes on to proclaim that they – *will be called priests of the Lord, and named ministers of our God* (Isaiah 61:6). Every born-again believer is commissioned and anointed to rebuild, restore and renew through the anointing upon them, as Jesus did.

ANOINTED TO REBUILD, RESTORE & RENEW

He restores my soul (Psalm 23:3).

Rebuild, restore and renew have the following meanings.

Rebuild – Build again or differently.
Restore – Give back to the original owner; make restitution; reinstate; bring back to dignity or right.
Renew – Revive; regenerate; make new again; restore to the original state; recover one's youth, strength.

We saw earlier, that the Anointing oil was sacred and had a unique formula – no other oil had the same ingredients. When we operate in the Anointing of God, we are in a realm like nothing else on earth. Therefore, it is important that we do not seek to copy worldly patterns, or tamper with the principles of God's Word. It would be like trying to change His instructions. *He has anointed us* (2 Cor. 1:21), and therefore equipped us to minister to people in a completely unique way – His way.

Jesus told His disciples – *The words I have spoken to you are spirit and they are life* (John 6:63). His words are not ordinary words. They are not only wise; they are literally life-forming.

*The first man Adam became a living being**; the last Adam (Christ Jesus), a life-giving spirit*** (1 Corinthians 15:45).

We are anointed to *rebuild*, *restore* and *renew* (Isaiah 61:1-4). We do so, according to the principles of God's Word – *"Not by might, nor by power,* ***but by my Spirit****,"* says the Lord Almighty (Zechariah 4:6). The Word and the Spirit work as one.

Therefore, let us realise the incredible potential that is within every born-again believer, and move in the power of the Anointing that we have received through Christ Jesus.

CHAPTER THIRTY-ONE

FULFILLING SCRIPTURE - AUTHORITY

Jesus said, "Today this Scripture is fulfilled in your hearing" (Luke 4:21).

Jesus said the above words in the synagogue at the beginning of His public ministry. He had just read aloud a portion of Scripture from Isaiah, concerning The Anointing.

*The Spirit of the Lord is on me, because **He has anointed me** to preach good news to the poor. He has sent me to proclaim freedom for the prisoners and recovery of sight for the blind, to release the oppressed, to proclaim the year of the Lord's favour* (Luke 4:18-19; Isaiah 61:1-2).

He announced that He was the fulfilment of the words recorded in Isaiah; and also declared that they were going to see Him fulfil the ministry to people, as recorded in that passage of Scripture. They would see *Scripture fulfilled* in their midst.

Jesus made the above statement because He was completely sure of the words spoken, and that He had the power and authority to fulfil them. There are numerous examples throughout Scripture where Jesus did something, which was followed by the statement – *that it might be fulfilled.*

One such example of this is the incident where Jesus healed Peter's mother-in-law, drove out the spirits from the demon-possessed, and healed all the sick (Matt. 8:14-16). We see a scripture from the New Testament (Matt. 8:17) recording the fulfilment of another from the Old (Isaiah 53:4).

This was to fulfil what was spoken through the prophet Isaiah*: "He took up our infirmities and carried our diseases"* (Matthew 8:17).

CHRIST'S AMBASSADORS

We are Christ's ambassadors, as though God were making His appeal through us (2 Corinthians 5:20).

An ambassador means: 'a diplomatic official appointed and accredited as a representative in residence by one nation to another; an authorised messenger or representative; one who stands for or represents a set of values' (Universal Dictionary).

When we are born again, God *brings us into the Kingdom of the Son He loves* (Col. 1:13). We become an ambassador of Christ. We are a representative of His Kingdom on earth.

We are *Christ's ambassadors* to take the *message of reconciliation* to the world (2 Cor. 5:19). Jesus testified – *The Spirit of the Lord is on me, because* **He has anointed me to preach good news to the poor** (Luke 4:18). The Lord has now commissioned us to do likewise (Matt. 28:18-19).

As defined above, an ambassador 'stands for and represents a set of values.' In this second part of the book, we are examining discipleship, and how to *know Him (Christ) better* (Eph. 1:17). We discover the reality of *holding to the Lord's teaching* (John 8:31). As we *hold* to the 'set of values' that God's Word declares, we will inevitably experience pressure to collapse. But, an ambassador is commissioned to 'stand.'

When an ambassador is appointed, he is given a seal of approval; he is 'an authorised messenger and representative.' When we are born again, becoming *Christ's ambassadors* (2 Cor. 5:20), we also are given a seal – *Having believed,* **you were marked in Him with a seal, the promised Holy Spirit** (Eph. 1:13). The Spirit is the *seal* that we receive, which is the authorisation to be a 'messenger and representative' of the Kingdom of God, and to fulfil all the duties of such a position.

AUTHORISATION

***Jesus said, "All authority in Heaven and on earth has been given to me. Therefore go** and make disciples of all nations"* (Matthew 28:18-19).

There were a number of occasions during Jesus' ministry when He sent out His disciples to do the same things that He did.

When Jesus had called the Twelve together, **He gave them power and authority** *to drive out all demons and to cure diseases, and He sent them out to preach the Kingdom of God and to heal the sick* (Luke 9:1-2).

Prior to the Lord's ascension into Heaven, He told His disciples of the power that would come upon them by the Spirit:

*"Do not leave Jerusalem, but wait for the gift my Father promised, which you have heard me speak about. For John baptised with water, but in a few days you will be baptised with the Holy Spirit...**You will receive power when the Holy Spirit comes on you; and you will be my witnesses**...to the ends of the earth"* (Acts 1:4-8).

We receive His resurrection life within us – *He who raised Christ from the dead will also give life to your mortal bodies* ***through His Spirit, who lives in you*** (Rom. 8:11).

The Lord wants us to be true *ambassadors* for Him by living like Him. He told us – *I tell you the truth, anyone who has faith in me will do what I have been doing* (John 14:12). What did Jesus do when He was on earth?

God anointed Jesus of Nazareth with the Holy Spirit and power, and ***He went around doing good and healing all who were under the power of the devil*** (Acts 10:38).

TESTIMONIES

Paul and Barnabas spent considerable time there, speaking boldly for the Lord, who **confirmed the message of His grace by enabling them to do miraculous signs and wonders** (Acts 14:3).

We began this chapter by looking at Jesus' declaration – *Today this Scripture is fulfilled in your hearing* (Luke 4:21). The more that we *hold to His teaching* (John 8:31), the greater will be the amount of testimonies *of His grace* (Acts 14:3) that we experience in our life. In a similar manner to that of the Lord we openly declare to others, "Because of Christ within me, today this Scripture is fulfilled in your midst."

For example, if we are facing a difficult situation, we *hold* to what His Word teaches, irrespective of the circumstances – *The peace of God, which transcends all understanding, will guard your hearts and your minds in Christ Jesus* (Phil. 4:7). We can respond to His Word by applying His peace to our lives – *Let the peace of Christ rule in your hearts* (Col. 3:15). When people ask us how we remain so calm, we can say – "Through Christ within me, today this Scripture (Phil. 4:7) is fulfilled in your midst."

When we speak a *spiritual truth in spiritual words* (1 Cor. 2:13) that *sets the captive free* (Isaiah 61:1-3), we are in effect declaring – "Through Christ's anointing, which He has placed in me (2 Cor. 1:21), today this Scripture (Isaiah 61:1) is fulfilled."

The above verse (Acts 14:3) states that Paul and Barnabas *spoke boldly for the Lord*. As an *ambassador for Christ* (2 Cor. 5:20), we are called to speak boldly for Him. Jesus *healed all who were under the power of the devil* (Acts 10:38). We are authorised and empowered by the Lord to do the same – *They overcame him (the devil) by the Blood of the Lamb and* **by the word of their testimony** (Rev. 12:11). We can fulfil Scripture.

CHAPTER THIRTY-TWO

FULFILLING SCRIPTURE – SPIRIT AND LIFE

Your word, O Lord, is eternal; it stands firm in the Heavens (Psalm 119:89).

The Word of God will never lose its power and authority. It *stands firm*, irrespective of circumstances, because it is *eternal*. In order to *fulfil* His Word in our lives and the situations that we face, it has to *remain in us* (John 15:7). We have to keep *hold* of it (John 8:31).

*Jesus said, "If you remain in me and **my words remain in you**, ask whatever you wish, and it will be given you. This is to my Father's glory, that you bear much fruit, showing yourselves to be my disciples"* (John 15:7-8).

In the Parable of the Sower (Luke 8:1-15), three-quarters of the *seed* (Word of God) that went into the peoples' lives did not have the effect it was meant to have, because it did not *remain*. One quarter was snatched away almost immediately; the second quarter did not take proper root because of lack of depth; the third quarter subsequently got choked by life's worries, riches and pleasures, not maturing.

It was only one portion that *remained* rooted firmly in good soil, stood the test of time, and then produced a good crop.

Jesus said, **"The words I have spoken to you are spirit and they are life"** (John 6:63). That is an established fact. But we will not encounter the reality unless His words *remain in us*.

Every Christian has the capacity to *fulfil Scripture* (Luke 4:21) by obeying His Word. We experience His *seed* maturing in us, which produces fruit. The key to doing so is to take *hold*, and then keep *hold* of the *seed*, so that it *remains* firmly rooted.

PENTECOST

*Peter stood up with the Eleven, raised his voice and addressed the crowd: "Let me explain this to you...**This is what was spoken by the prophet Joel**"* (Acts 2:14-16).

When Peter addressed the crowd on the day of Pentecost, he stated that what had just happened to the disciples was Scripture being *fulfilled*. He was saying to them, "Today this Scripture (Joel 2:28-32) is fulfilled in your midst," namely – *I will pour out my Spirit on all people* (Joel 2:28).

Prior to His ascension, Jesus told His disciples not to leave Jerusalem; to *wait for the gift my Father promised* (Acts 1:4). What do you think took place in the upper room during those days when the disciples were waiting? It is significant that it states – ***And afterwards**, I will pour out my Spirit* (Joel 2:28).

The two words *and afterwards* obviously refers to something happening that subsequently led up to the outpouring of the Holy Spirit. God said through Joel: *Return to me with all your heart* (v.12); *rend your heart* (v.13); *call a sacred assembly* (v.15); *the promise of new wine* (v.19); *they will be full* (Joel 2:12-26).

When Peter referred to the second part of Joel's prophesy he knew that the disciples had already *fulfilled* the first part. They had *returned to the Lord with all their heart*, the gathering in the upper room was a *sacred assembly*; they had consecrated their lives to the Lord. They had repented of previous failings, and settled any selfish ambition, personality conflicts and jealousies that had arisen between them in the past. They were ready.

When they were filled with the Spirit, they knew that the ***and afterwards*** had come – *vats were overflowing with new wine* (Joel 2:24). Scripture was *fulfilled*, because they were obedient; the *seed* (Word) had entered them, and *remained* in good soil.

EXPECTATION

*May the God of hope fill you with all joy and peace as you trust in Him, so that you may **overflow with hope** by the power of the Holy Spirit* (Romans 15:13).

The Scriptural meaning of hope is – 'a favourable and confident expectation; a happy anticipation of good.' When Jesus told the disciples to *wait for the gift my Father promised* (Acts 1:4), they were full of expectancy. In those forty days prior to the Lord's ascension, He had *spoken about the Kingdom of God* (Acts 1:3). They were *overflowing with hope* (Rom. 15:13), having 'a favourable and confident expectation.'

Scripture being *fulfilled* is linked with expectation. God is faithful; He is true to His Word. Therefore, we can be confident of a positive outcome when we *hold onto* (John 8:31) His Word. We do not take it for granted, have a disrespectful attitude, or simply assume that things will happen. Instead, we remain faithfully expectant of a 'happy anticipation of good.'

*Faith is being **sure of what we hope for** and certain of what we do not see* (Hebrews 11:1).

Faith (Greek 'pistis') means – 'a firm persuasion.' We saw earlier that hope ('elpis') means – 'a favourable and confident expectation.' Therefore, the literal translation of the first part of Hebrews 11:1 is – 'Having a firm persuasion of a confident and favourable expectation; a happy anticipation of good.'

The Word of God is the 'logos' and 'rhema.' Receiving a 'rhema word' is when the Spirit brings a particular Scripture to our mind, that we are to then *hold onto* in order to see it *fulfilled* in our life, or that of others. We stand on the particular word with expectancy, because we know that *His Word will achieve the purpose for which He sent it* (Isaiah 55:11).

SUDDENLY

When the day of Pentecost came, they were all together in one place. **Suddenly** *a sound like the blowing of a violent wind came from Heaven and filled the whole house where they were sitting* (Acts 2:1-2).

At Pentecost, the disciples were prepared and ready for the '*suddenly*,' whatever would happen. They had lined themselves up with the Word of God in order to see Jesus' words *fulfilled*. They probably did not know the exact outcome of their preparation; but they did know with certainty that something was going to happen. The reason they knew this was because Jesus had told them, and they *waited* (Acts 1:4) in obedience.

There is a direct link between faith and obedience. It reveals that we are preparing ourselves for a 'suddenly.' The Spirit takes us further into our inheritance; to explore the Kingdom of God.

As has been stated previously in this book, God's love is unconditional; we cannot earn it. But in order to come into all the inheritance that He has for us whilst we are on earth, then it requires that we do something about it.

God is omniscient; meaning that He is all knowing. He created time on earth, He Himself, is outside of that time. Therefore, He is aware of when we are ready for a 'suddenly.' It is no surprise to Him; He is waiting for us. We get ready by *holding onto* His Word – *"The words I have spoken to you are spirit and they are life"* (John 6:63). They are literally life-changing. By *holding onto* them, we will see *Scripture fulfilled* in our life, family, work, church etc.

We confidently *wait* for the '*suddenly*' to occur – *Now to Him who is able to do immeasurably more than all we ask or imagine,* ***according to His power at work within us*** (Eph. 3:20).

CHAPTER THIRTY-THREE

FULFILLING SCRIPTURE - RESTING

The message they heard was of no value to them, because those who heard did not combine it with faith (Hebrews 4:2).

The Lord God told the Israelites that He was going to lead them out of bondage in Egypt, into *a land flowing with milk and honey* (Ex. 3:8; 4:29-31). Sadly, a generation failed to encounter that promise because of their rebellion and unbelief. It was only Joshua and Caleb's family that experienced the *fulfilment* of God's word to that generation, because they were men of faith - *Without faith it is impossible to please God* (Heb. 11:6).

Scripture records many examples of people who hear the same message, but not all receive it by faith.

*Paul went to the synagogue on three Sabbath days to reason with them from the Scriptures, explaining and proving that the Christ had to suffer and rise from the dead...**Some of the Jews were persuaded** and joined Paul and Silas, as did a large number of God-fearing Greeks* (Acts 17:2-4).

His Word remains true. He never goes back on His covenant promise. But those who experience it are those who believe it.

The principle of hearing God's Word, and combining it with faith, applies not only to being born again, but also to how we continue in our relationship with the Lord. The Israelites did not come into the *rest* (Heb. 4:3) that God had for them. It was open to all of them; every one of them could have entered. But they failed to see *Scripture fulfilled* (Luke 4:21) because of unbelief.

As born-again believers, God has called us into His *Sabbath-rest* (Heb. 4:9), and all the promises that His *rest* entails. These promises are *fulfilled* in us as we combine them with faith.

HARDENING OUR HEARTS

*See to it that none of you has a sinful, unbelieving heart that turns away from the living God...Today, if you hear His voice, **do not harden your hearts*** (Hebrews 3:12-15).

We saw in the previous chapter, that receiving a 'rhema word' is when the Holy Spirit gives us a particular Scripture verse or passage to *hold onto* (John 8:31) in order to see it *fulfilled* in our life, or that of others. One of the reasons why we may fail to hold onto the word is the unbelief caused by a hardened heart. It can become hardened by such things as continual sin, or doubt, fear or worry being *stored* in our heart.

*Jesus said, "**Out of the overflow of the heart** the mouth speaks. The good man brings good things out of the good **stored up in him**, and the evil man brings evil things out of the evil stored up in him"* (Matthew 12:34-35).

Jesus explained that our spiritual heart is our storehouse. The condition of our heart is therefore vitally important. What we think about each day will form the content of our heart; the place where our attitudes take shape, either for the good or bad. The words that we speak come from what is *stored* in us – *Above all else, **guard your heart** for it is the wellspring of life* (Prov. 4:23).

If we are seeking to see *Scripture fulfilled* in our life it is vital that we do not allow our heart to become hardened, because this will cause unbelief to nullify our faith. If this happens it will become evident in our words. We will find ourselves thinking and declaring "It will never happen" or "I am tired of waiting."

The more that we watch our thoughts, the more we will *guard our heart*, and *hold onto* His Word by faith, irrespective of circumstances – ***Whatever happens**, conduct yourselves in a manner worthy of the gospel of Christ* (Phil. 1:27).

A DISCIPLE'S HEART

The Word of God *is living and active. Sharper than any two-edged sword, it penetrates even to dividing soul and spirit...**it judges the thoughts and attitudes of the heart*** (Hebrews 4:12).

The first part of Hebrews chapter four explains how the Israelites did not come into the inheritance that God had provided, because of their unbelief. Their hearts had become hardened; consequently, they did not encounter fulfilment.

The chapter then reveals that *the thoughts and attitudes of our heart are judged by the Word of God* (Heb. 4:12). It does so by *dividing our soul and spirit.*

Our spirit will always be in line with the Word of God, because the Lord Jesus resides there by the Holy Spirit, who is *the mind of Christ* (1 Cor. 2:16) within us. When we are born again, *our spirit is alive because of (Christ's) righteousness* (Rom. 8:10). Therefore, the 'thoughts' that come from our spirit will be those of the Lord.

Our soul, which comprises of our mind, heart emotions, conscience, will, temperament, character and personality is different. It is in the process of being restored. It is subject to fluctuation. That is why our heart, even after becoming a Christian, can become hardened through doubt, fear etc.

The Lord knows the condition of our mind and heart – **You perceive my thoughts from afar**...*Before a word is on my tongue you know it completely, O Lord* (Psalm 139:2-4).

A disciple's heart, although not perfect, will increasingly *store* (Matt. 12:35) the principles of the Word of God, which the Holy Spirit will help us combine with faith.

THE RESTING PLACE

There remains a Sabbath-rest for the people of God; *for anyone who enters God's rest also rests from his own work, just as God did from His. Let us, therefore, make every effort to enter that rest, so that no-one will fall by following their (the Israelite's) example of disobedience* (Hebrews 4:9-11).

The complete *fulfilment* of our *rest* in God will occur in eternity. But His *rest* is also for us now.

God created the world in six days. He then rested on the seventh – *God blessed the seventh day and made it holy, because on it* ***He rested from all the work of creating*** *that He had done* (Gen. 2:3). The word *rest* (Hebrew – sabat) means 'ceasing from work because it is complete' (Vine's expository). He did not rest because He was tired. *Rest* means that it was finished.

In the above verses (Heb. 4:9-11) the *Sabbath-rest* (Greek – sabbatismos) is the 'rest' of God Himself (Vine's). When we enter into relationship with the Father through the Lord Jesus, we enter into His *rest*. We cease from our work, which is based upon our self-effort. We 'rest/repose' (katapausis) in Him.

Jesus compared the *rest* (Greek – anapausis) that He gives with that of the religious rulers at that time. Their perception of being at rest was the self-satisfaction of obedience to their rules and regulations; whereas, the *rest* that Jesus gives is based upon relationship. It means 'cessation from work; refreshment' (Vine's). He brings peace – *Come to me, all you who are weary and burdened, and* ***I will give you rest*** (Matt. 11:28).

When we seek to experience *Scripture being fulfilled* in our life, or that of the others, we do so from a place of *rest* in Him. Our *fulfilment* comes from our relationship with Him. It is from that resting place that we *fulfil* the works that He has for us.

CHAPTER THIRTY-FOUR

GRACE & WORKS

*For it is by grace you have been saved, through faith – and this not from yourselves, it is the gift of God – **not by works**, so that no-one can boast* (Ephesians 2:8-9).

One of the hindrances to *knowing Him (Christ) better* (Eph. 1:17) is straying away from God's grace (His unmerited favour) into our own works. From the world's perspective, Paul had every reason to put confidence in his own ability, and self-effort:

*If anyone else thinks he has reasons to put confidence in the flesh, I have more: circumcised on the eighth day, of the people of Israel, of the tribe of Israel, of the tribe of Benjamin, a Hebrew of Hebrews; in regard to the Law, a Pharisee; as for zeal, persecuting the church; **as for legalistic righteousness, faultless*** (Philippians 3:4-5).

After being born again, Paul could have returned to past habits of self-effort because of his driven and performance-related nature. He had many natural talents, and was well-versed in religious teaching. Thankfully, he did not return to past ways because he had revelation of the grace of God. He spoke very directly to the Galatian Church who had started out so well, but were returning to legalism and a works mentality.

You who are trying to be justified by law have been alienated from Christ; you have fallen away from grace (Galatians 5:4)

In chapter four, we examined the central doctrines that bring us into, and then keep us in relationship with the Father: namely justified; reconciled; redeemed; adopted; glorified; sanctified. It is only through Jesus' finished work at the Cross that this has been made possible – ***The Law was put in charge to lead us to Christ that we might be justified by faith*** (Gal. 3:24).

HAGAR OR SARAH

*Abraham had two sons, one by the slave woman (Hagar) and the other by the free woman (Sarah)...These things may be taken figuratively...**Now Hagar stands for Mount Sinai in Arabia and corresponds to the present city of Jerusalem, because she is in slavery with her children**. But the Jerusalem that is above is free (Sarah), and she is our mother* (Galatians 4:22-26).

Paul revealed that, figuratively speaking, Hagar represented Mount Sinai, where the Law was given. Many in Jerusalem were, sadly, still living under it; but – *Christ redeemed us from the curse of the Law by becoming a curse for us* (Gal. 3:13).

Paul stated that when we are born again it comes from the *Jerusalem that is above, and is free* (Gal. 4:26). Our spiritual birth is from Heaven – *As is the man from Heaven (Christ), so also are those who are of Heaven* (1 Cor. 15:48). Having been born again by the Holy Spirit, we are then to live our lives by the Spirit. We cannot relate to God in any other way. If we try to live under the Law with a works mentality after having been born again of the Spirit, then there will be conflict in our lives.

*Now you, like Isaac (son of Sarah), are children of promise. At that time **the son born in the ordinary way (Ishmael, son of Hagar) persecuted the son born by the power of the Spirit**. It is the same now* (Galatians 4:28-29).

We will not be able to *know Him (Christ) better* (Eph. 1:17) by trying to live according to a law mentality, with a works and performance mind-set. Paul reminded them and us today, to eliminate that type of thinking. We are in relationship with Him through the Spirit – *What does the Scripture say? Get rid of the slave woman and her son, for **the slave woman's son will never share in the inheritance with the free woman's son*** (Gal. 4:30).

LIVING IN GRACE

The life I live in the body, I live by faith in the Son of God, who loved me and gave Himself for me. ***I do not set aside the grace of God****, for if righteousness could be gained through the Law, Christ died for nothing!* (Galatians 2:20-21).

Paul stated – *I do not set aside the grace of God* (Gal. 2:21). He was emphatic about this because he knew that if we do so, we will lapse back into a 'gospel' that is based upon legalism, and our self-effort. He confronted the Galatians:

I am astonished that you are so quickly deserting the one who called you by the grace of Christ and are turning to a different gospel – ***which is really no gospel at all*** (Galatians 1:6-7).

When we are born again, we receive God's grace, knowing that we cannot earn our salvation – *For it is* ***by grace you have been saved, through faith****; and this not from yourselves it is the gift of God* (Eph. 2:8). We initially believe it; but after time passes, we can, at times, fall back into a works mentality; thinking that we have to maintain righteousness by human effort.

Did you receive the Spirit by observing the Law, or by believing what you heard? ***After beginning with the Spirit, are you now trying to attain your goal by human effort?*** (Galatians 3:2-3).

The *renewing of our mind* (Rom. 12:1-2), that we examined in chapters twenty-seven to twenty-nine, is the re-shaping of our thoughts to the Word of God. Paul *renewed his mind* to live in grace, not by works; ***he did not set aside the grace of God***. He knew that it was only by Christ's righteousness within him (Rom. 8:10) that he was in relationship with the Father. He kept his mind *renewed* to this truth, living in the grace of God.

GOOD WORKS WHICH GOD PREPARED

We are God's workmanship, created in Christ Jesus to do **good works, which God prepared in advance for us to do** (Ephesians 2:10).

Paul first of all sets out the principle upon which we receive our salvation – *Because of His great love for us, God, who is rich in mercy,* **made us alive with Christ** *even when we were dead in transgressions –* **it is by grace you have been saved** (Eph. 2:4-5).

Just in case we do not grasp it the first time, Paul re-emphasises that it is by grace, and not works – **It is by grace you have been saved, through faith** *– and this not from yourselves, it is the gift of God – not by works, so that no-one can boast* (Eph. 2:8-9).

In that *place of rest* (Heb. 4:1-11), that we looked at in the previous chapter, where we are *renewing our mind* (Rom. 12:2) according to the Word of God, and *living by the Spirit* (Gal.5:25), we are able to hear clearly from the Lord the things that He wants us to do; His good works, not ours – **the good works, which God prepared in advance for us to do** (Eph. 2:10).

This does not mean that everything has to be perfect in our life. Because of His grace, God will use us even when we are in a weak or vulnerable state; Scripture is full of individuals that He used in such circumstances.

But in order to consistently hear from Him, His Word declares that we are to *renew our mind* according to His mind – **Then you will be able to test and approve what God's will is** *– His good, pleasing and perfect will* (Rom. 12:2). We abandon our self-righteousness and self-effort, and come before Him in humility through His righteousness, and listen for His direction.

CHAPTER THIRTY-FIVE

THE TRIAL OF OUR FAITH

Consider it pure joy whenever you face trials of many kinds, because you know that the testing of your faith develops perseverance (James 1:2-3).

Before we are born again, we have little or no perception of the spiritual dimension that exists in our life, and in the world around us; or the consequences of certain thoughts or actions. Our understanding of faith is that of a 'belief system.'

It is only when we become a Christian that we are able to discern spiritual matters. We discover that our faith is not a belief system of rules and regulations; it is a relationship with a person, the Lord Jesus. He speaks to us through His Word and Spirit; we are thereby able to understand all that pertains to faith.

The man without the Spirit does not accept the things that come from the Spirit of God, for they are foolishness to him, and he cannot understand them, because **they are spiritually discerned** (1 Corinthians 2:14).

We have the assurance – *Never will I leave you; never will I forsake you* (Heb. 13:5); the Holy Spirit *lives in you* (Rom. 8:11). In order to function and fulfil God's purposes in our life, every believer is given *the measure of faith* (Rom. 12:3). What happens to that faith afterwards is our responsibility. His Spirit within us will always seek to teach and guide us (John 16:13-15); but we co-operate with Him by applying faith.

Our faith is not meant to 'gather dust.' It is for constant use in order to see victory in *all kinds of trials* (1 Peter 1:6).

These have come so that your faith; of greater worth than gold…may be proved genuine (1 Peter 1:7).

The Trial of our Faith

PERSEVERANCE

***Perseverance must finish its work** so that you may be mature and complete, not lacking anything* (James 1:4).

Perseverance means – 'The holding to a course of action, belief, or purpose without giving way; steadfastness.' It would be true to say that perseverance is not the best loved word. We would prefer words like blessing, inheritance and abundance. But *perseverance* is a vital aspect of our maturing in the Lord.

James 1:2 states – *Consider it pure joy whenever you face trials of many kinds*. We saw earlier from 1 Corinthians 2:14 that the man without the Spirit of God cannot understand the things of God – *They are foolishness to him*. Such a person would think it inconceivable that someone would *consider it pure joy to face trials*. They believe that trials bring sadness. Such matters are **spiritually discerned** (1 Cor. 2:14).

In addition, they do not have the *fruit of the Spirit* (Gal. 5:22-23) in their life. Every believer has *joy*, which is part of the *fruit*, and is therefore within us. It is not like the joy that the world experiences, which is based on favourable circumstances. A born again believer's *joy* is something of substance, not fleeting.

That *joy* enables us to *know that the testing of our faith develops perseverance* (James 1:2). Through *holding to the Word* (John 8:31), and with the help of the Spirit within us, we are able to persevere, knowing that **perseverance produces character** (Rom. 5:4). (We will be examining character in the following chapter).

Our faith is *of greater worth than gold* (1 Peter 1:7). When we hold on, without giving way, we are able to remain steadfast *– **our faith is proved genuine** and results in praise, glory and honour when Jesus Christ is revealed* (1 Peter 1:7).

TESTS

*Blessed is the man who perseveres under trial, because **when he has stood the test**, he will receive the crown of life that God has promised to those who love Him* (James 1:12).

The evangelist Joyce Meyer says, 'If we want to have a testimony then we have to go through a test.' We each have a testimony when we *hold to the Word* (John 8:31), irrespective of our circumstances. In so doing, we defeat the devil who seeks to undermine our faith by every means – *They overcame Satan by the blood of the Lamb and by **the word of their testimony*** (Rev. 12:11). We persevere in order to *stand the test* of our faith.

Before becoming a Christian we do not understand that there is The Kingdom of God, and a kingdom of darkness.

*Having disarmed the powers and authorities, **Jesus made a public spectacle of them**, triumphing over them by the Cross* (Colossians 2:15).

Jesus made *a public spectacle* of the defeat of Satan's powers and authorities. Scripture informs us that – *Our struggle is not against flesh and blood, but against the rulers, against the authorities, against the powers of this dark world* (Eph. 6:12). When we overcome *the spiritual forces of evil in heavenly realms*, we are fulfilling what the Lord has enabled us to do by His *anointing* (2 Cor. 1:21), which is in us. We *stand our ground* (Eph. 6:13). In defeating *Satan's schemes* (2 Cor. 2:11) we are continuing to make a *public spectacle* of the devil's defeat.

We also defeat the devil even in the seemingly minor issues in life. Satan endeavours to get inroads into our soul through our mind, trying to *outwit us* (2 Cor. 2:11) through such things as worry, fear and doubt. But we continue to overcome him by *holding onto the Word*, thereby seeing victory come to pass.

SUFFERING

*I want to know Christ...and **the fellowship of sharing in His sufferings*** (Philippians 3:10).

The Father does not put suffering upon a Christian. His wrath was placed upon Christ at the Cross – **God did not appoint us to suffer wrath but to receive salvation** (1 Thess. 5:9). He does not put suffering upon us to teach us something; He uses His Word for this – *All Scripture is God-breathed and is useful for teaching, rebuking, correcting and training* (2 Tim. 3:16).

What were the sufferings of Christ? It was prophesied of Jesus that – *He was despised and rejected by men, a man of sorrows, and **familiar with suffering*** (Isaiah 53:3). Throughout His earthly life, He encountered all manner of opposition from religious leaders, and others who would not accept Him. At the Cross, Jesus suffered and died for the sins of the world. The Apostles, Paul and Peter, revealed that there is a dying to self, and sin, that every believer *suffers*, as we identify with the Lord.

*I have been crucified with Christ and **I no longer live, but Christ lives in me**. The life I live in the body, I live by faith in the Son of God, who loved me and gave Himself for me* (Galatians 2:20).

*If you suffer for doing good and you endure it, this is commendable before God. To this you were called, because **Christ suffered for you, leaving you an example**, that you should follow in His steps* (1 Peter 2:20-21).

The *suffering* that we experience is living a consecrated life, denying ourselves. We choose to live according to God's Word, irrespective of the consequences. Jesus revealed the cost of being a disciple – *If anyone would come after me, he must deny himself and **take up his cross and follow me*** (Matt. 16:24).

CHAPTER THIRTY-SIX

CHARACTER

We rejoice in the hope of the glory of God. Not only so, but we also rejoice in our sufferings, because we know that **suffering produces perseverance; perseverance, character;** *and character, hope* (Romans 5:2-4).

Character is the combination of qualities or features that distinguishes one person from another; the moral or ethical nature of a person. It is built upon the values and convictions that we have embraced over the years.

Before we become a Christian we can possess many good qualities, and lead a moral and upright life, having a certain degree of strength of character.

The difference that occurs after we are born again is that our strength of character is not built upon our own self, with our own set of values. It is founded upon the nature and character of our Father. We then live and accomplish things in His strength, according to His ways, because we *participate in His nature.*

His divine power has given us everything we need for life and Godliness...He has given us His very great and precious promises so that through them ***you may participate in the divine nature*** (2 Peter 1:3-4).

The way that we build Godly character into our life is through His Word, and by maturing in the fruit of the Spirit – *love, joy, peace, patience, kindness, goodness, faithfulness, gentleness and self-control* (Gal. 5:22). These grow within us as we *live by the Spirit, and keep in step with the Spirit* (Gal. 5:25).

There are no short cuts to developing character. 'You can mould a mannerism but you must chisel a character' (Prochnow)

THOUGHTS & CHARACTER

*Whatever is noble, right, pure, lovely, admirable – if anything is excellent or praiseworthy – **think about such things*** (Philippians 4:8).

Our character is **revealed** in times of difficulty and success, but it is **formed** in our daily living. What do we think about each day? What are the seeds that we are planting on a daily basis? We will reap the harvest from the type of seed that we plant. The substance of what we think will be that which we sow into our lives. It will produce an outcome whether for the good or bad.

The essence of what Scripture teaches concerning the effect of our thoughts on our character is described as follows:

> Watch your **thoughts**; they become your words.
> Watch your words; they become your actions.
> Watch your actions; they become your habits.
> Watch your habits; they become your **character**.
> Watch your character; it shapes your destiny.
> (Frank Outlaw)

Our character has a great deal of influence upon our successes and failures. But it all begins with the thoughts that we dwell on each day, as we saw earlier in chapters twenty-seven to twenty-nine, concerning the renewing of our mind. Where we are in life, whether spiritually, emotionally, and even physically can be traced back to what we have dwelt upon in our mind – ***As a man thinks in his heart so he is*** (Prov. 23:7 King James).

It is abundantly clear from reading the Word of God that the Apostle Paul had developed Godly strength of character. How did he achieve it? He practised *capturing his thoughts* (2 Cor. 10:5) and *renewing his mind* (Rom. 12:2) each day – *Whatever you have learned from me...**put it into practice*** (Phil. 4:9).

CONSCIENCE & CHARACTER

*I strive always to **keep my conscience clear** before God and man* (Acts 24:16).

Our conscience and character are meant to work in harmony with one another. As we saw in chapter twenty-one, our conscience does not govern what we believe. It reacts to the values and principles that we have already accepted; the opinions and attitudes that we believe and endorse. It responds to the content of our character, whether it is good or bad.

When we are born again, both our conscience and character undergo a transformation as our natural mind is *renewed* (Rom. 12:2) according to the *mind of Christ* (1 Cor. 2:16) within us, which is the Holy Spirit. We learn to – ***put off the old self and put on the new self*** (Eph. 4:22-24).

A born-again believer's character is shaped by the *fruit of the Spirit* (Gal. 5:22-23). In so doing, our conscience becomes more sensitive to each aspect of the *fruit*. For example, as we grow in *self-control*, our conscience will 'notify' us if we are not living in the right manner concerning it. We then respond accordingly.

Our spirit is that part of us where the Holy Spirit resides. It is from there that He speaks. He teaches us the Word of God, and guides us in life. He is that 'inner voice' within us.

Our spirit, conscience and character can function together in harmony. Paul revealed to us the way that it affects our everyday life. He *kept his conscience clear* (Acts 24:16), so that he was not affected by any guilt and condemnation. His character was built upon the Word of God; and he listened to the guiding of the Holy Spirit within his spirit – *My conscience confirms it in the Holy Spirit* (Rom. 9:1). His character was sound; his conscience was sensitive; and he also 'checked things out' with the Spirit.

DEVELOPING STRENGTH OF CHARACTER

I do not run like a man running aimlessly; I do not fight like a man beating the air. No, I beat my body and make it my slave (1 Corinthians 9:26-27).

We saw earlier that *perseverance produces character* (Rom. 5:4). In the above verse, Paul gives us insight into how he was so effective; how he had *persevered* to develop strength of character in order to cope with whatever he faced.

He explained that to 'last the distance' in a race we need to train continually – **Everyone who competes in the games goes into strict training**. *They do it to get a crown that will not last; but we do it to get a crown that will last forever* (1 Cor. 9:25).

Developing strength of character is a daily experience. It has to be approached in a way that an athlete or boxer disciplines himself in preparation for a race or a fight. When the time comes for it to be tested, he is in a state of readiness.

'Character is built into the spiritual fabric of personality hour by hour, day by day, year by year in much the same deliberate way that physical health is built into the body' (Lamar Kincaid).

Scripture states that **character produces hope** (Rom. 5:4). We need hope to use faith – *Now faith is being sure of what we hope for* (Heb. 11:1). We can therefore see the importance of character. If our character is not strengthened, it will be weak; which means that our hope is not firm; and our faith cannot then function properly. But when our character is strong in God's principles we are ready to accomplish great things for His glory.

Daniel **so distinguished himself** *among the administrators and the satraps* **by his exceptional qualities** *that the king planned to set him over the whole kingdom* (Daniel 6:3).

CHAPTER THIRTY-SEVEN

STANDING

Put on the whole armour of God, so that when the day of evil comes, **you may be able to stand your ground, and after you have done everything, to stand** (Ephesians 6:13).

In the previous chapter we examined the importance of developing a Godly character so that we become more like Christ Jesus; having the strength of character to *stand our ground*, and fulfil His purposes for our life.

When we are born again we are given a suit of *armour* to wear (Eph. 6:14-18). It is noticeable that Scripture encourages us to **put on the whole armour of God**, not just certain parts, in order to *stand our ground*. For the purpose of understanding, Paul compared it to what a soldier of his day would be wearing.

The belt of truth – we are secure in the truth of God's Word: **the breastplate of righteousness** – we are in right-standing with God because of Christ's righteousness that He has given us; His protection is upon us: **shoes** – brass shoes were used to prevent soldiers from treading on sharp sticks, which would render them unable to march and advance; we are called to take the Gospel everywhere: **the shield of faith** – throughout our life the devil will aim all manner of temptation, fear and doubt at us; but we extinguish all his flaming arrows by holding up our shield of faith, the truth of God's Word: **the helmet of salvation** – we are saved through Christ Jesus; no-one can snatch us out of our Father's hand; our hope and faith are in Him: **the sword of the Spirit** – the five previous pieces of armour are for protection; the sword is the Word of God by which we go on the offensive by believing and declaring the Word.

When we, like a soldier, *put on the armour* and use it, we are able to *stand our ground* and also support those around us.

STAND FIRM

Be on your guard; **stand firm in the faith**; *be men of courage; be strong* (1 Corinthians 16:13).

There are times in life where we find it difficult to *stand firm in the faith* because we are 'weak in our knees.' This happens through such things as sustained pressure, sickness, over-work or worry etc. How do we regain strength to stand firm again?

Strengthen your feeble arms and weak knees! *Make level paths for your feet, so that the lame may not be disabled, but rather healed* (Hebrews 12:12-13).

Spiritually, our *'arms and knees'* become weak when we are standing or walking on 'rough and rocky ground.' Scripture tells us to – *make level paths for your feet* (Heb. 12:13). How do we make level paths so that we can *stand firm*? We prepare the way for the Lord, to stand on His ground.

Isaiah revealed that John the Baptist would *prepare the way* for Jesus (Isaiah 40:3). Today, we also prepare the way for the Lord to change our life by making the rough places smooth – **The rough ground shall become level**, *the rugged places a plain, and the glory of the Lord will be revealed* (Isaiah 40:4).

When Isaiah heard a voice telling him to "Cry out," he asked what he should say. He was told, *"The grass withers and the flowers fall, but* **the Word of our God stands for ever***"* (Isaiah 40:6-8). We prepare the way for the Lord by standing upon what His Word declares; we *stand* on His *level ground*.

After Jesus had chosen the twelve apostles, *He went down with them and* **stood on a level place** (Luke 6:17), where He ministered in word and healing. It was as if the Lord was saying, "With me, you shall always stand firm on level ground."

STANDING TOGETHER

Whatever happens, *conduct yourselves in a manner worthy of the Gospel of Christ. Then, whether I come and see you or only hear about you in my absence, I will know that you **stand firm in the one Spirit, striving together as one** for the faith of the Gospel* (Philippians 1:27).

All born-again believers are joined together in the Lord – *You are the body of Christ, and each one of you is a part of it* (1 Cor. 12:27). The *body* is meant to function in such a way that, through its unity, we support one another – *There should be no division in the body, but its parts should have **equal concern for each other*** (1 Cor. 12:25).

The early Church knew how to function ***together*** – *When the day of Pentecost came, they were **all together** in one place* (Acts 2:1): *All the believers were **together** and had everything in common* (Acts 2:44): *Every day they continued to meet **together** in the temple courts. They broke bread in their homes and ate **together** with glad and sincere hearts* (Acts 2:46).

The pattern of present-day life has changed from those early-Church days. Because of work commitments etc it is impractical for us to meet every day in large numbers. But there are certain principles that ought to remain, such as *standing firm in one spirit, striving together as one*; close fellowship, regularly meeting in one another's homes; breaking bread together.

Paul valued *partnership* with the Philippians (Phil. 1:5). He could rely on them – *It was good of you to share in my troubles* (Phil 4:14). They *stood firm* with him, just like Philemon.

Your love has given me great joy and encouragement, *because you, brother, have refreshed the hearts of the saints* (Philemon 7).

STANDING ALONE

Each one should carry his own load (Galatians 6:5).

As previously stated, every believer is in the *body of Christ* (1 Cor. 12:27), and as such we are to support one another. But this does not mean that we are to live a life of dependence upon others, whether it is family, the pastor, elders, or friends. We ought to be able to *carry our own load*, spiritually, emotionally and physically. Obviously, there are certain exceptions.

Paul encouraged individuals to take responsibility for themselves – *Each one should test his own actions* (Gal. 6:4); but at the same time be willing to both give and receive help from others – *carry each other's burdens* (Gal. 6:2). We are to *fulfil the law of Christ* (Gal. 6:2), which is the law of love. When individuals can function independently of others, and yet also be joined together in unity and support with fellow believers, then the body of Christ is greatly strengthened.

Paul knew the support of others; but he was also able to stand alone. He had a very challenging experience at the end of his life – *At my first defence, no-one came to my support, but* ***everyone deserted me***. *May it not be held against them* (2 Tim. 4:16). Sometimes we can feel isolated. It can be through the insensitivity of fellow believers, or our own actions. How did Paul react to being *deserted*?

> ***The Lord stood at my side and gave me strength***, *so that through me the message might be fully proclaimed*
> (2 Timothy 4:17).

Paul stood on what God said – *Never will I leave you; never will I forsake you* (Deut. 31:6). He knew it to be true, and therefore he was at peace in the most trying of circumstances. He was able to **stand** because he knew the Lord **stood** at his side.

CHAPTER THIRTY-EIGHT

NO TURNING BACK

*On hearing it, many of His disciples said, "This is a hard teaching. Who can accept it?"...**From this time many of His disciples turned back and no longer followed Him*** (John 6:60-66).

The previous day, Jesus had fed the five thousand with five loaves and two fishes (John 6:1-15). The crowd followed Him across the lake, wanting to hear and see more of the Lord.

*They asked Jesus, "What must we do to do the works God requires? Jesus answered, "The work of God is this**: to believe in the One He has sent**"* (John 6:28-29).

Jesus told them that He is *the bread of life* (John 6:35). The Jews took offence at this, because they did not believe that He was the One that God had sent. Jesus then emphasised the point by saying, *"I am the living bread that came down from Heaven. If anyone eats of this bread, he will live for ever. **This bread is my flesh, which I give for the life of the world**"* (John 6:51).

This caused further discussion amongst the hearers, until Jesus brought the matter to a head by saying, *"**Whoever eats my flesh and drinks my blood remains in me, and I in him**. Just as the living Father sent me and I live because of the Father, so the one who feeds on me will live because of me"* (John 6:56-57).

Jesus sought to take the people further on in the revelation of who He is. But they did not grasp the significance of His words. The Jews did not accept Him, and sadly, even some of His own followers *found it a hard teaching. Who can accept it?* (John 6:60). They had previously believed the Lord's words, and had experienced the miraculous. But at the point of going deeper in Him they *turned back*. They were only content to go so far.

NO LOOKING BACK

*Jesus said, "No-one who puts his hand to the plough **and looks back** is fit for service in the Kingdom of God"*
(Luke 9:62).

Jesus compared *service in the Kingdom of God* to that of ploughing a field, in preparation for the sowing of seed. When someone is engaged in ploughing, it is important that they keep their eyes focussed on the ground ahead. If they look back, they will cut a ridge between the furrows rendering it unsuitable for the planting of seed.

If we want to be of *service* to the Lord, we need to 'plough the ground' in such a manner that our eyes are firmly focussed ahead, being led by His Spirit; not looking back to our old ways of doing things. When we plough a straight course, we prepare the ground for the seed – *the Word of God*.

*Jesus said, "This is the meaning of the Parable (of the Sower): **The seed is the Word of God**"* (Luke 8:11).

As Christians we have probably all had moments when we have *looked back*, through taking our eyes off the Lord and His Word. Fortunately, by His grace, we get back on track within a short space of time. If, however, we continue to look back, then, although we may be in the Kingdom of God, we will certainly not be *fit for service in the Kingdom* (Luke 9:62).

*The eyes of the Lord range throughout the earth to strengthen those **whose hearts are fully committed to Him***
(2 Chronicles 16:9).

There is a cost in following Jesus - **commitment**. His Word declares that He is looking for people who will not look back; but who are *fully committed* to Him, looking forward.

FORMER THINGS

One thing I do: ***forgetting what is behind and straining towards what is ahead****, I press on towards the goal to win the prize for which God has called me Heavenwards in Christ Jesus* (Philippians 3:13-14).

Scripture informs us that the devil is a thief (John 10:10). If we do not *renew our mind* (Rom. 12:1-2), and *guard our heart* (Prov. 4:23), we will allow the devil to influence our thoughts, whereby we are robbed of fulfilment in the present, because we are bound up with regrets from the past. It is not God's purpose for us to be held captive to guilt and condemnation (Rom. 8:1-4).

There are some things that we cannot alter. However, there are certain occasions where we do need to correct past sins or mistakes, in order to put matters right with someone that we may have offended; and hopefully see the relationship restored. But with the Lord, there is no point in trying to 'make it up to Him.' We cannot repay Him for anything we did prior to, or after becoming a Christian. He has brought us into His *eternal redemption* (Heb. 9:12). This does not mean that we take His forgiveness for granted; it simply means that we humble ourselves, and continue to change to become more like Him.

In addition to past mistakes, there is also the danger of becoming captive to former blessings. Scripture warns of the futility of dwelling on such matters – ***Forget the former things: do not dwell on the past. See, I am doing a new thing*** (Isaiah 43:18-19). It is good to remember and praise God for what He has done previously; but He does not want us *dwelling on the past*, and in so doing, miss Him *doing a new thing* in the present.

Paul did not let anything hold him captive. He did not *dwell on* that which was good or bad from the past. He continued to *press on,* heading forward, fulfilling God's purposes for his life.

HEADING FORWARD

"You do not want to leave too, do you?" Jesus asked the Twelve. Simon Peter answered Him, "Lord, to whom shall we go? You have the words of eternal life. **We believe and know** *that you are the Holy One of God"* (John 6:67-69).

Jesus asked this question immediately after the incident when – *many of His disciples turned back and no longer followed Him* (John 6:66). Peter gave that wonderful reply to Him – *"You have the words of eternal life"* (John 6:68).

It is interesting to examine the next words that Peter spoke – **We believe and know** (John 6:69). The disciples that remained had passed from *believing* to *knowing*. They had matured in their relationship with Jesus. For them, there was no *turning back*, because as Peter rightly said, *"Lord, to whom shall we go?"*

The ones who turned back had **believed** in part, but they did not **know** *the Holy One of God* (John 6:69). Peter and the other Eleven knew that there was no turning back because, having tasted of the living Word, the Lord Jesus, there is nowhere else to go in life. They wanted to head forward, following Jesus.

Jesus said, "If you hold to my teaching, you are really my disciples. Then you will **know the truth***, and* **the truth will set you free***"* (John 8:31-32).

As we are nearing the end of Part Two, having examined aspects of *knowing* the Lord Jesus, it is worth each of us reflecting upon our relationship with Him. Can we truly say that we have passed from *believing* to *knowing*? Has the Word of God become more than just good words – **the one who feeds on me will live because of me** (John 6:57). Do we *hold to His Word* irrespective of our circumstances? If so, then we will experience what the Lord promised would follow – *freedom* (John 8:32).

CHAPTER THIRTY-NINE

FREEDOM

It is for freedom that Christ has set us free (Galatians 5:1).

When we mature in the Lord, from *believing* to *knowing*, one of the most significant things that we notice is the *freedom* that we encounter. We are no longer held captive to guilt, condemnation, worry, fear, doubt or consciousness of the approval of others. This does not mean that we are oblivious or totally unconcerned about other people; but it does mean that our mind is no longer shaped by outside circumstances.

Do not conform any longer to the pattern of this world, but **be transformed by the renewing of your mind** (Romans 12:2).

Our soul consists of our mind, heart, emotions, will, conscience, temperament, character and personality. We have seen previously that our mind is the entrance to our soul; what enters through it affects all the other parts. Therefore, if our mind is free, the rest of our soul will encounter freedom.

In the above verse (Gal. 5:1), Paul informed the Galatian Church of the *freedom* that we have in Christ, and then encouraged them to – *Stand firm, then, and* **do not let yourselves** *be burdened again by a yoke of slavery* (Gal. 5:1).

Every believer has received that *freedom* in Christ within our spirit, where the Lord resides by the Holy Spirit (John 3:6; Rom. 8:10). But in order for us to experience that freedom within our soulish realm we have to *capture our thoughts* (2 Cor. 10:5), and *renew our mind* (Rom. 12:2), so that we – **do not let yourselves** *be burdened again by a yoke of slavery* (Gal. 5:1). Scripture tells us that we are the ones who *let* such things happen. It is our choice as to whether we live in the *freedom* that the Lord gives.

FREEDOM FROM CONDEMNATION

Therefore, ***there is now no condemnation for those who are in Christ Jesus****, because through Christ Jesus the law of the Spirit of life set me free from the law of sin and death* (Romans 8:1-2).

Christians *believe* the above verses; but do we really *know* them? Has that *seed* (Luke 8:11) penetrated into good soil within our lives, so that we can testify that we are consistently experiencing its fruit? Have we taken *hold of it* (John 8:31), *meditated upon it* (Joshua 1:8), *reflected* (2 Tim. 2:7), and *applied it* (Prov. 23:12)? This means that its truth has grown within us; the *seed* has become *the stalk, then the ear, then the full grain in the ear* (Mark 4:28).

There are two laws at work – *the law of the Spirit of life and the law of sin and death* (Rom. 8:2). Scripture informs us that we have been *set free* from the law of sin and death. The new covenant of **the law of the Spirit** is **superior to the old one** (Heb. 8:6). It is established in the Kingdom of God; it is not going to be over-turned. But we have a choice to make; what law are we going to live under? If we dip in and out between the old and the new, we will inevitably experience condemnation because we inflict it upon ourselves. It does not have to be that way.

In chapter thirty, we examined the Anointing that we receive at the time of our salvation – *He anointed us* (2 Cor. 1:21); *you have an anointing from the Holy One...the anointing you received from Him remains in you* (1 John 2:20; 27).

The anointing that *we receive from the Lord remains* (1 John 2:27) in us. One aspect of the anointing is to – **proclaim freedom for the captives** (Isaiah 61:1). Through His anointing within us, together with standing firm upon the Word of God, we are no longer held captive to guilt and condemnation. We are free.

FREEDOM FROM FEAR

Fear of man will prove to be a snare, *but whoever trusts in the Lord is kept safe* (Proverbs 29:25).

There are many forms of fear. One of the major ones that still affect Christians is the fear of man; whether it is of the leadership in work or church, or concern as to what others think. So often, it occurs because the person is living under the law of the old covenant, having a works mentality, which seeks the approval of others, and thereby it pressurises them to 'perform.' It arises from pride; having a fear of rejection or condemnation if they do not please others. Paul did not fear what man thought.

*We are not trying to please men but God, who tests our hearts...**We were not looking for praise from men**, not from you or anyone else* (1 Thessalonians 2:4-6).

We are not meant to have an 'island' mentality (Rom. 14:7); being oblivious to what people think. But equally, our thoughts and attitudes are not to be held captive to the opinions of others. We are joined together in *the body of Christ* (1 Cor. 12:27); but we are answerable first and foremost to the Head, who is Christ. We put God's Word above man's thoughts.

Scripture encourages us to *submit to one another out of reverence for Christ* (Eph. 5:21). Submission has to do with the attitude of our heart. However, although we may submit to someone out of respect, it does not necessarily mean that we are to obey them. It depends on their instructions, as to whether it complies with God's Word. Do we have that inner witness?

The more that we meditate upon God's Word, and develop sensitivity to the Spirit, the easier it becomes to instinctively *know* that which is right. We learn to value the guidance and encouragement of others; but not to be governed by them.

FREE TO EXPLORE

The land we passed through and explored is exceedingly good (Numbers 14:7).

When we are born again, we enter the Kingdom of God (1 Thess. 2:12; Col. 1:13). Sadly, what can so often happen is that, having entered, we just remain around the entrance, and do not *explore* any further. The Lord Jesus wants to take us by the hand, and by His Spirit, take us on a journey of discovery.

One of the reasons that we do not progress is that we are continually resolving 'issues' within our life; or our spiritual development is restricted by dealing with guilt and condemnation; or we have a lack of understanding of our identity in Christ – *You are no longer a slave, but a son; and since you are a son,* **God has made you also an heir** (Gal. 4:7).

The only way to overcome such matters is to *take hold of His Word* (John 8:31) and mature in Him by *believing* and *knowing* its truth (2 Tim. 1:12). Having *known the truth, the truth will set us free* (John 8:31). There are no short cuts, it is by endurance.

Everything that was written in the past was written to teach us, so that **through endurance and the encouragement of the Scriptures** *we might have hope* (Romans 15:4).

Freedom is a great blessing; but it is also for our *service in the Kingdom of God* (Luke 9:62). In that verse, Jesus told us that *anyone who looks back is unfit for service*. One of the evidences of true *freedom* in the Lord is that a person does not choose to look back. They have *renewed their mind* in His Word to the extent that it does not enter their thoughts. Their attention is no longer centred upon themselves. They are *free* to focus on that which is ahead, in *service* for Him, whether it is witnessing, gifting, ministry, prayer etc. They are ready for expansion.

CHAPTER FORTY

FREEDOM TO EXPAND

Enlarge the place of your tent, stretch your tent curtains wide, **do not hold back**; *lengthen your cords, strengthen your stakes* (Isaiah 54:2).

Isaiah chapter 53 is a prophetic statement concerning the sacrificial death of Jesus – *pierced for our transgressions* (Isaiah 53:5). This is followed by a prophecy of His Church that He will establish – *They will spread out to the right and to the left* (Isaiah 54:3). The chapter declares that the central truth upon which His Church will be built is Christ's own righteousness, that He imputes into every born-again believer – *In righteousness you will be established* (Isaiah 54:14).

We are a people who have been *called into His Kingdom and glory* (1 Thess. 2:12). Our relationship with our Father is based solely on Christ's righteousness within us; our works cannot achieve this before, or after our salvation. We receive His righteousness *by His grace through faith* (Eph. 2:8).

Having entered into relationship, we desire to respond to Him in both a spiritual and practical manner. In other words, we have great blessing, but also great responsibility – *We are God's workmanship, created in Christ Jesus to do good works, which God* **prepared in advance for us to do** (Eph. 2:10).

Isaiah progressively reveals Christ Jesus: chapter 53 – His sacrifice; chapter 54 – His Church established; chapter 55 begins with the invitation – *"Come, all you who are thirsty."*

We can therefore see why Isaiah 54 begins with the encouragement to *enlarge the place of your tent*. It is to make room for people – *descendants* (Isaiah 54:3) Our Father encourages each of us – **do not hold back** (Isaiah 54:2).

STRETCH YOUR TENT CURTAINS WIDE (Isaiah 54:2)

Is our vision limited? If so, then Scripture encourages us to *stretch our tent curtains wide* in order to get a bigger picture of what is around us. The Lord Jesus desires to give continual revelation of Himself to us, both individually and collectively. Our response is to seek and watch for revelation, in order that we get understanding of how we can be used to do His will, and see His Kingdom grow – *Your Kingdom come, your will be done on earth as it is in Heaven* (Matt. 6:10).

> *I will stand at my watch and station myself on the ramparts;* ***I will look to see what He will say to me****...Write down the revelation and make it plain on tablets so that a herald may run with it* (Habakkuk 2:1-2).

When we *stretch our curtains wide* we are also able to see the needs that are around us, and respond accordingly. Not only are we able to see outwards, but we also allow the world to look in and discover that our lives are open. We are declaring God's Word – *"Come, all you who are thirsty"* (Isaiah 55:1). We invite them into our *'tent.'* We make room for them in our lives.

> *For I was hungry and you gave me something to eat, I was thirsty and you gave me something to drink, I was a stranger and you invited me in, I needed clothes and you clothed me, I was sick and you looked after me, I was in prison and you came to visit me...**I tell you the truth, whatever you did for one of the least of these brothers of mine, you did for me*** (Matthew 25:35-40).

It is clear from the above Scriptures that there is a spiritual and a physical application of *stretching our tent curtains wide*. When we do so, we are making a declaration that our eyes are focussed on that which really matters. We are looking out, and also allowing others to look inside, thereby revealing the Lord.

Freedom to Expand

LENGTHEN YOUR CORDS (Isaiah 54:2)

When we *enlarge the place of our tent* it is necessary to *lengthen our cords*. In doing so, we are making a statement that we are preparing for expansion. We are saying that we have seen the potential for growth, and we are actively responding for that to happen. We are not restricting expansion within our lives.

If the lengths of the cords attached to the tent are too short, the structure will be unstable. When something increases in size, the cords have to be *lengthened*. They need to be the right length, and correctly positioned in the ground.

When we seek to expand in the Lord Jesus in both revelation and doing His will, how do we find the right way?

Your Word *is a lamp to my feet and a light for my path* (Psalm 119:105).
When He, **the Spirit** *of truth, comes, He will guide you into all truth* (John 16:13).

Symbolically, the *cords* (guide-ropes as they are known today) is the work of the Holy Spirit, and the *stakes* to which they are attached is the Word of God. The Word and the Spirit function together; they are always attached to one another. We have a sure confidence when we know that the *'tent'* in which we live is securely held in place by the *cords* and the *stakes*.

We *lengthen our cords* by asking the Holy Spirit to enlarge our understanding, and to guide us in preparing for expansion – **He will guide you into all truth** (John 16:13). He guides us to where the *stakes* are to be placed.

Every believer is a *'tent'* in God's Kingdom (2 Peter 1:13). We are not called to live in a restricted space – *All over the world this Gospel is bearing fruit and* **growing** (Col. 1:6).

STRENGTHEN YOUR STAKES (Isaiah 54:2)

If the stakes, to which the cords are attached, are not strong, then the tent's structure will not remain stable and secure, it will be vulnerable to the wind and rain that 'attack' it. We are the same in our *tents* (2 Peter 1:13). When we are secured firmly by strong *stakes* (The Word of God), and *cords* (The Holy Spirit), then our *'tent'* will stand, and not be blown over by the pressures of life, or the spiritual attacks of the devil.

> *I will always remind you of these things, even though you know them…I think it right to refresh your memory as long as I live in* **the tent of this body** (2 Peter 1:12-13).

Abraham believed the words that God spoke to Him. He stood on them, holding fast, and saw them come to fruition.

> *Abraham did not waver through unbelief regarding the promise of God, but was* **strengthened in his faith** *and gave glory to God,* **being fully persuaded** *that God had power to do what He had promised* (Romans 4:20-21).

The Psalmist also knew where his strength came from – **strengthen me according to your Word** (Psalm 119:28). Paul said the same thing – *Faith comes by hearing, and hearing by the Word of God* (Rom. 10:17 King James translation).

> *Just as you received Christ Jesus as Lord, continue to live in Him, rooted and built up in Him,* **strengthened in the faith as you were taught** (Colossians 2:6-7).

God told Joshua – *Do not let this (Word) depart from your mouth;* **meditate upon it day and night** (Joshua 1:8). We are the same. We *strengthen our stakes* when we meditate and continually remind ourselves of the truth of His Word. Our *'tent'* will then be strong enough for every challenge that we face.

CHAPTER FORTY-ONE

CONVINCED

I am convinced that neither death nor life, neither angels nor demons, neither the present nor the future, nor any powers, neither height nor depth, nor anything else in all creation, will be able to separate us from the love of God that is in Christ Jesus our Lord (Romans 8:38-39).

Paul told Timothy – *I know whom I have believed, and am* **convinced** (2 Tim. 1:12). He had undergone the transformation of going from *believing* in the Lord; to *knowing* Him and the truth of His Word; to the point where He was *convinced*.

The transformation that took place in Paul was remarkable. When he appeared before King Agrippa, he described the complete change that had taken place in his life. Paul told him that formerly – *I too was convinced that I ought to do all that was possible to oppose the name of Jesus* (Acts 26:9).

Prior to coming into relationship with the Lord Jesus, Paul was captive to *legalistic righteousness* (Phil. 3:6). He was so convinced of his *faultlessness* (Phil. 3:6) in His 'performance' that he became ever more self-righteous, justifying his own actions, believing that he was keeping the Law.

However, when he was born again, he went from *believing*, to *knowing*, to then being *convinced* as a result of having a personal relationship with a person, the Lord Jesus. Formerly, he was convinced by his perceived self-righteousness; but after becoming a Christian, he became *convinced* through *Christ's righteousness within Him* (Rom. 8:10) – a complete reversal.

How do we become **convinced**? Paul discovered that it was not by self-effort. It was by *knowing* the reality of God's love for us through the abiding presence of the Lord Jesus, by His Spirit.

NEITHER DEATH NOR LIFE, ANGELS NOR DEMONS

*I eagerly expect and hope...that now as always Christ will be exalted in my body, **whether by life or by death**. For to me, to live is Christ and to die is gain* (Philippians 1:20-21).

Paul's attitude to life and death had been *transformed by the renewing of his mind* (Rom. 12:2). The world no longer had any hold upon him, because he had *set his mind and heart on things above, not on earthly things* (Col. 3:1-2). His relationship with Christ Jesus was so close that it mattered not whether he served the Lord on earth, or went to be with Him in eternity. The reason that Paul was so **convinced** is that he had come to *believe* and *know* the truth of the following:

He who unites himself with the Lord is one with Him in spirit (1 Corinthians 6:17).

The meaning of the above verse is that the Lord, with those who accept Him, literally become one entity. This reveals the incredible grace of God, that He would join Himself completely with us through the Lord Jesus. Paul had revelation of this, and it transformed his thinking, and therefore his manner of living.

The security that Paul knew in Christ Jesus enabled him to state that no *angels or demons could separate him from the love of God* (Rom. 8:38). God's angels obviously would not seek to separate. But there are fallen angels – *God did not spare angels when they sinned, but sent them to hell...to be held for judgement* (2 Peter 2:4). They have no authority over a believer.

The same applies to demons. There is nothing to fear; the disciples declared – *Lord, even the demons submit to us **in your name*** (Luke 10:17). Paul also operated in the Lord's authority over all things demonic. He was **convinced** that he was able to, because he was *one in spirit with the Lord*.

NEITHER THE PRESENT, THE FUTURE NOR POWERS

> *God anointed us, set His seal of ownership on us, and put His Spirit in our hearts as a deposit,* **guaranteeing what is to come** (2 Corinthians 1:21-22).

When we become a Christian, God anoints us with the Holy Spirit – *His seal of ownership*. The Spirit who comes to live within us is not only for the present time – *Never will I leave you; never will I forsake you* (Heb. 13:5); but He is also a *guarantee of what is to come*. We have become *one in spirit with the Lord* (1 Cor. 6:17), past, present and future. Therefore, Paul was **convinced** that whatever he encountered in life, God's love would never depart from him. He could face anything.

> *I consider that our present sufferings are not worth comparing with the glory that will be revealed in us* (Romans 8:18).

The above verse (Rom. 8:18) reveals *the glory that will be revealed in us*. This is not only referring to eternity. It will happen in the present and future, whilst we are still on earth, as we honour the Lord in our daily living – *We are being transformed into Christ's likeness with* **ever-increasing glory**, *which comes from the Lord, who is the Spirit* (2 Cor. 3:18).

Paul also revealed that *no powers can separate us from the love of God*. He informed the Ephesian Church:

> *For our struggle is not against flesh and blood, but against the rulers, against the authorities,* **against the powers of this dark world and against the spiritual forces of evil in the heavenly realms** (Ephesians 6:12).

When we *put on the full armour of God* that He gives us, we are able to *stand our ground* (Eph. 6:13), **convinced** of victory.

NEITHER HEIGHT NOR DEPTH, OR ANYTHING ELSE

I know what it is to be in need, and I know what it is to have plenty. ***I have learned the secret of being content in any and every situation****, whether well fed or hungry, whether living in plenty or in want. I can do everything through Him (Christ Jesus) who gives me strength* (Philippians 4:12-13).

In the above verse, Paul revealed some of the heights and depths that he had encountered. The key part is when he says – *I have learned the secret of being content in any and every situation*. He had undergone the transformation of **believing** that he could be *content*; to **knowing** the means by which he was able to continually apply it to events; to finally being **convinced** of the fact, because it was tried and tested within his life.

Paul explained that becoming *content* in both the heights and the depths is not something that happens over-night; it is **learned** over a period of time. He trained himself in this area because he was *convinced* that he could *do everything through Christ who gives him strength* (Phil. 4:13). It is the same for us.

When Paul is describing God's love towards us in his letter to the Roman Church, he gets to a point as if he is lost for words in trying to describe such matters; so he makes an all encompassing statement – ***nor anything else in all creation****, will be able to separate us from the love of God that is in Christ Jesus our Lord* (Rom. 8:39).

Every Christian faces challenges in life, both spiritual and physical. God has enabled us to be *more than conquerors through Him who loved us* (Rom. 8:37). Sometimes, we see the immediate victory; at other times there is a passage of time. But however long it takes, we have *the strength to get through everything* (Phil. 4:13) when we, like Paul, are **convinced** of God's continual love towards us, through Christ Jesus.

CHAPTER FORTY-TWO

FIRMLY ESTABLISHED

*I will always remind you of these things, even though you know them and are **firmly established in the truth you now have*** (2 Peter 1:12).

According to present-day surveys, many people are 'dippers' – they do not remain with one book, reading it from cover to cover; instead, they 'dip into' one or several at the same time. There is nothing wrong with this form of reading; each of us manage our time, or pattern of living that suits us.

But when it comes to the Word of God, we will not become *firmly established in the truth* (2 Peter 1:12) if we are 'dippers.' If we 'dip in and out' of His Word, not only in our reading of Scripture, but also in our dwelling and meditating upon it, then we will not fully grasp its truth, or mature in our faith.

The Holy Spirit gave revelation to Paul concerning the six fundamental doctrines of the Word of God – *justified* (Gal. 2:16); *reconciled* (2 Cor. 5:19); *redeemed* (Rom. 3:24); *adopted* (Gal. 4:5-7); *sanctified* (1 Cor. 6:11); *glorified* (Rom. 8:30).

The early church was taught these doctrines, in order that they became *firmly established in the truth* (2 Peter 1:12). Paul encouraged Timothy: ***Continue in what you have learned and have become convinced of*** (2 Tim. 3:14).

Work and family commitments can, at certain times, make it difficult to find space to study God's Word. But each one of us can learn to meditate; to 'chew over' a verse, or passage of Scripture each day; allowing the Holy Spirit to teach us. This is part of the process of *renewing our mind* (Rom. 12:1-2). If we *train ourselves* in these matters on a daily basis, it will assist us in becoming ***firmly established in the truth*** (2 Peter 1:12).

HOLDING ONTO THE WORD

***Anyone who listens to the Word but does not do what it says** is like a man who looks at his face in a mirror and, after looking at himself, goes away and immediately forgets what he looks like* (James 1:23-24).

When we examine the Word of God, listen to a preacher, read a book, or get revelation directly from the Holy Spirit, what is our response? Do we say to ourselves – "I'll give that a try?" However, as the weeks and months pass, we do not *hold onto the truth*, and let it slip from our grasp. We may return to it at a later time, and again 'give it a try,' but never really grasp its truth.

Looking back over our lives, would it be fair to say that we have 'dipped in and out' of truth? This question is not to bring guilt and condemnation, but that we be honest with ourselves.

We can *believe* something from God's Word, but unless we *train ourselves* in *holding onto its truth*, we will not *know it with certainty* in our own life. The principle of going from *believing*, to *knowing*, to then becoming *convinced* (2 Tim. 1:12) can be applied to all the truths of His Word.

If we remain 'dippers' into Scripture, instead of meditating upon its truth, then we will find that we often 'give something a try,' but do not see it come to fruition. It can be compared to the Parable of the Sower – the seed does not produce real growth.

They receive the Word with joy when they hear it, but they have no root. ***They believe for a while***, *but in the time of testing they fall away* (Luke 8:13).

The Lord does not want us to *believe for a while*. He desires that – *His seed sprouts and grows…producing the stalk, then the ear, then the full grain in the ear* (Mark 4:27-28).

KNOWING WITH CERTAINTY

> *"Now they know that everything you have given me comes from you. For I gave them the words you gave me and they accepted them.* **They knew with certainty** *that I came from you, and* **they believed** *that you sent me"* (John 17:7-8).

In Jesus' prayer to the Father, just before His crucifixion, He stated that His disciples had gone from *believing*, to *knowing with certainty*; being convinced. They temporarily panicked at the time of His death, but they re-formed quickly. They obeyed what the Lord told them, and *waited* (Acts 1:4) with expectation.

What caused His disciples to pass from *believing,* to then *knowing with certainty*? Jesus gives us the answer – *I gave them the words you gave me and* ***they accepted them*** (John 17:8).

To *accept* something is to willingly receive it. Jesus rejoiced that His disciples had chosen to follow Him. They had not turned back, as those described in John 6:60-66. The reason for their continuing is given by Peter – *"Lord, to whom shall we go?* ***You have the words of eternal life. We believe and know*** *that you are the Holy One of God"* (John 6:68-69). They had *accepted* His words; not a notional acceptance, but rather a *knowing with certainty*. They had taken them into their lives.

When Paul said *I am convinced* (Rom. 8:38), he used the word 'peitho,' meaning – 'persuaded, won over, bringing about a change of mind.' Like the disciples, he was persuaded and won over because of his relationship with the Lord. He accepted His words – **he believed, and knew them with certainty**. Abraham, also, was fully assured ('plerophoreo') of God's word to him.

> *Abraham did not waver through unbelief regarding the promise of God...* ***being fully persuaded*** *that God had power to do what He had promised* (Romans 4:20-21).

TRAINED IN GODLINESS

*Solid food is for the mature, who **by constant use have trained themselves*** (Hebrews 5:14).

When an athlete prepares for a contest, he does not 'dip in and out' of training. If he did so, he would not be match-fit. It is the same in the spiritual. Paul revealed his training schedule.

*Everyone who competes in the games goes into strict training...Therefore **I do not run like a man running aimlessly**; I do not fight like a man beating the air. No, I beat my body and make it my slave* (1 Corinthians 9:25-27).

As we saw previously, Paul was a man of the Spirit (1 Cor. 2 10-16). He knew that the most important part of him was his spirit, where the Lord Jesus resides within us by the Holy Spirit (John 3:5-6; Rom. 8:10). Through *training himself to be Godly* (1 Tim. 4:7), Paul brought his soul and body in line with his spirit. He did not allow 'feelings' to get in the way – *I beat my body and make it my slave* (1 Cor. 9:27).

Paul decided that he was not going to *run like a man running aimlessly* (1 Cor. 9:26). There was nothing aimless about his manner of living. He *knew with certainty* (John 17:8). He *constantly trained himself* (Heb. 5:14) in *holding onto the Word* (John 8:31). Paul was not a 'dipper' in the Word of God. He grasped the truth, being diligent in his witness for the Lord.

Be diligent in these matters; give yourself wholly to them**, so that everyone may see your progress. Watch your life and doctrine closely. **Persevere in them (1 Timothy 4:15-16).

Perseverance is not the most popular of words. However, it produces *character* (Rom. 5:4), which we all need in order to remain ***firmly established in the truth*** (2 Peter 1:12).

CHAPTER FORTY-THREE

CONFIDENCE

Blessed is the man who trusts in the Lord, whose confidence is in Him. *He will be like a tree planted by the water that sends out its roots by the stream. It does not fear when heat comes; its leaves are always green. It has no worries in a year of drought, and never fails to bear fruit* (Jeremiah 17:7-8).

When we mature in our faith, from *believing* to *knowing*, to then becoming *convinced*, we develop a greater degree of confidence, which affects all aspects of our life.

Confidence means – 'assurance and certainty; a trusting relationship.' We saw in chapter forty-one that, prior to his salvation, Paul's confidence was based upon his own works and performance. But after being saved, his confidence was no longer governed by his own ability, and self-righteous attitude; it was through his relationship with the Lord – ***I can do everything through Him*** *(Christ Jesus) who gives me strength* (Phil. 4:13).

Confidence also means – 'that which enables one to stand, endure, have a foundation.' The above Scripture (Jer. 17:7-8) reveals that, when our *confidence is in the Lord*, we are able to stand and endure because He is our foundation – *we will not fear when heat comes…nor worry in a year of drought* (Jer. 17:8). We stand upon the truth of His Word, confident of the outcome.

The Word and the Spirit function together. When we are firmly rooted in God's Word, *we send out our roots by the stream* (Jer. 17:8) of the Holy Spirit. This means that even in the most challenging and testing of times, we can still *bear fruit*.

I am confident of this, *that He who began a good work in you will carry it on to completion* (Philippians 1:6).

APPROACHING GOD WITH CONFIDENCE

In Christ and through faith in Him **we may approach God with freedom and confidence** (Ephesians 3:12).

How confident are we in approaching God at all times? We can *believe* that Jesus has made it possible; we may also *know* it to a certain degree; but are we *convinced* of its truth? Have we *renewed our mind* (Rom. 12:1-2), so that we have eliminated a works and performance mentality? If we still have such a mindset, it will hinder our *freedom and confidence in approaching God*; the reason being that we cannot offer any sacrifice on our part; it is only through Christ that we can approach the Father.

Christ entered the Most Holy Place once for all **by His own blood,** *having obtained eternal redemption* (Hebrews 9:12).

Paul was given revelation of the unity that a born-again believer has with the Father – *He who unites himself with the Lord is one with Him in spirit* (1 Cor. 6:17). This verse illustrates that the barrier of sin, that existed between man and God, has been completely removed through Christ – *God reconciled the world to Himself in Christ,* **not counting men's sins against them** (2 Cor. 5:19).

A condemned person does not have confidence; but, *there is now no condemnation for those who are in Christ Jesus* (Rom. 8:1). It is Christ's righteousness within our spirit that God sees when He looks at us – *Your spirit is alive because of (Christ's) righteousness* (Rom. 8:10). We may condemn ourselves, or we may encounter it from others; but we do not receive it from God.

We do not take His grace for granted (Rom. 6:1-2). But, in Christ, we can always be confident in approaching the Father – *Since we have a great High Priest...***let us approach the throne of grace with confidence** (Heb. 4:14-16).

CONFIDENCE IN OVERCOMING

*Though an army besiege me, my heart will not fear; though war break out against me, even then will I be confident...**I am still confident of this***: I will see the goodness of the Lord in the land of the living* (Psalm 27:3).

When we read the above Psalm, it is clearly evident that David was *convinced* that he would overcome whatever faced him; he therefore had *confidence*. He had trained himself to capture thoughts, as Paul described in 2 Corinthians 10:5. He captured that which would affect his confidence, and at the same time declared God's goodness towards him.

*The Lord is my light and my salvation – **whom shall I fear?** The Lord is the stronghold of my life – **of whom shall I be afraid?*** (Psalm 27:1).

When two fighters or sportsmen compete against one another, they look for signs of weakness in their opponent. If they can see any element of fear they become confident of gaining victory. The devil tries by all manner of means to intimidate us – *We are not unaware of his schemes* (2 Cor. 2:11). But, we have the ability, through Christ, to overcome.

Everyone born of God overcomes the world. *This is the victory that has overcome the world, even our faith. Who is it that overcomes the world? Only he who believes that Jesus is the Son of God* (1 John 5:4-5).

There are times in life when we do not feel an 'overcomer.' 1 John 5:5 asks the question – *Who is it that overcomes the world?* It then gives the answer – *He who believes that Jesus is the Son of God.* In other words, take our eyes off ourselves and our circumstances, and look to the One who is above all things – ***The Name that is above every name*** (Phil. 2:9).

THE PLACE OF CONFIDENCE

One thing I ask of the Lord, this is what I seek: that I may dwell in the house of the Lord all the days of my life, to gaze upon the beauty of the Lord and **to seek Him in His temple** (Psalm 27:4).

Throughout Psalm 27, David refers to facing opposition – *evil men advancing against him; enemies and foes attacking him* (v. 2); *an army besieging him, and war breaking out against him* (v. 3); *oppressors* (v. 11); *false witnesses rising up against him* (v. 12). What was his reaction to all that he faced?

My heart says of you, "Seek His face!" Your face, Lord, I will seek (Psalm 27:8).

Earlier, David had declared – *One thing I ask of the Lord, this is what I seek: that I may dwell in the house of the Lord...to seek Him in His temple* (Psalm 27:4). He declared that the answer to all that he faced was to be in the presence of the Lord.

Under the new covenant that Jesus established (Heb. 8:6), not only can *we approach the throne of grace with confidence* (Heb. 4:16) at all times, but also God has now entered us. Through Christ, we have become *the temple of the Holy Spirit* (1 Cor. 3:16: 6:19). Jesus told His disciples of what would happen after His ascension – *You know Him (Holy Spirit), for He lives with you and* **will be in you** (John 14:17). Through God's grace we are continually in fellowship with Him; we are able to receive strength and direction because of His presence within us.

The Lord wants us to live 'in confidence,' because His Word declares to us – **The One who is in you is greater than the one who is in the world** (1 John 4:4). Regardless of what we face in life, let us be *convinced* of His abiding presence within us, and therefore *confident* of overcoming all things through Him.

CHAPTER FORTY-FOUR

ASSURANCE

*Since I myself have carefully investigated everything from the beginning, it seemed good also to me to write an orderly account for you....**so that you may know the certainty of the things you have been taught*** (Luke 1:3-4).

At the outset of his Gospel, Luke explains his reason for writing – *so that you may know the certainty of the things you have been taught*. He wanted everyone who read it to have the same assurance that he had.

Assurance means – 'freedom from doubt; certainty; confidence; boldness; daring.'

Just before the Lord Jesus ascended into Heaven, He gave His commission to the disciples – **Surely I am with you always** (Matt. 28:20). He wanted them to *know the certainty* that, irrespective of circumstances, He would always be with them - *Never will I leave you: never will I forsake you* (Heb. 13:5).

In the insurance industry, there is a difference between 'insurance' and 'assurance.' For example, we insure our house regarding the possible event of damage or burglary; whereas in the case of our life-cover it is referred to as **assurance**, because our death is certain, as opposed to possible or probable.

The Lord wants His disciples to be certain in their faith. Instead of thinking 'possible or probable,' to have gone from *believing*, to *knowing*, to being *convinced*, so that they would *go and make disciples of all nations* (Matt. 28:19) with **assurance**; free from doubt, with certainty, confidence, boldness and daring.

That you may stand firm in all the will of God, ***mature and fully assured*** (Colossians 4:12).

ASSURANCE OF THE PAST

All of us who were baptised into Christ Jesus were baptised into His death. **We were therefore buried with Him through baptism into death** *in order that, just as Christ was raised from the dead through the glory of the Father,* **we too might live a new life** (Romans 6:3-4).

When we become a Christian, a 'baptism' takes place – *we are baptised into Christ*.

You are all sons of God through faith in Christ Jesus, for all of **you who were baptised into Christ** *have clothed yourselves with Christ* (Galatians 3:26-27).

When a Christian is physically baptised, the immersion under the water signifies that our 'old life' is dead, and the rising up out of the water declares that we have a 'new life' in Christ; who was crucified and died on the Cross; but who was then resurrected from the grave.

The Lord Jesus *reconciled* (2 Cor. 5:19) the world to the Father because of His *finished* (John 19:30) work on the Cross. We enter that *reconciliation* through Christ Jesus. Our salvation took place two thousand years ago; we enter it *by grace through faith* (Eph. 2:8), when we accept Jesus as our Lord and Saviour.

When we are born again, *the Holy Spirit* **gives birth** *to our spirit* (John 3:6). This means that our spirit is birthed *into Christ* making us one with Him – *He who unites himself with the Lord* **is one with Him in spirit** (1 Cor. 6:17).

We can be **assured** that our salvation is secure. When we become a Christian, our spirit is *sealed* (Eph. 1:13) by the Holy Spirit. Jesus declared, *"No-one can snatch them out of my hand"* (John 10:28). Our past is settled.

ASSURANCE FOR THE PRESENT

The Lord is my shepherd (Psalm 23:1).

When we read Psalm 23 it is clear that David had **assurance** of the abiding presence of the Lord God. He *believed* it, had got to *know* its reality by applying God's words to his life, and had thereby become *convinced* of God's love and faithfulness, irrespective of his circumstances. He *knew with certainty* (Luke 1:4); and that assurance affected all aspects of his life.

Even though I walk through the valley of the shadow of death, I will fear no evil, ***for you are with me*** (Psalm 23:4).

Jesus declared, *"I am the good shepherd"* (John 10:11). His sheep follow Him because – *they* ***know*** *His voice* (John 10:4). How do we get to *know* His voice? – It is through His Word and the teaching and guiding of His Spirit. Therefore, *those that have ears* (Matt. 11:15) can hear Him speak by His Spirit at all times; because He is ever-present.

God is our refuge and strength, an ***ever-present*** *help in trouble* (Psalm 46:1).

David knew God to be *ever-present*. Jesus established the new *covenant* (Heb. 8:6), by which we not only know His presence with us, but also in us – *You know Him (Holy Spirit), for He lives with you and* ***will be in you*** (John 14:17).

We have the **assurance** that we have God's presence within us at all times because, through Christ Jesus, we have become *the temple of the Holy Spirit* (1 Cor. 3:16; 6:19). From His continual presence within us, He speaks to us and guides us.

Jesus Christ is the same yesterday and today and for ever (Hebrews 13:8).

ASSURANCE FOR THE FUTURE

In my Father's house are many rooms; if it were not so, I would have told you... And if **I go and prepare a place for you***, I will come back and take you to be with me that you also may be where I am* (John 14:2-3).

The Lord Jesus has gone ahead to *prepare a place* for us in eternity. But He also goes ahead of us whilst we are still on earth, because He has *places* that He wants to take us, both spiritually and physically. The Lord has already gone ahead and *prepared* them; He then comes and takes us with Him. Each one of us can be **assured** that He has plans and purposes for us.

Before we go on a journey we pack a suitcase. Likewise, in order to go to those *places* that the Lord has prepared for us, let us pack our 'spiritual suitcase' full of His Word; to feed upon, meditate and declare its truth. In so doing, we prepare ourselves to get to those *place*, because *His Word will sustain us* (Psalm 119:116), and *His Spirit will guide us* (John 16:13).

The Lord God said to Jeremiah, *"Get yourself ready"* (Jer. 1:17). The reason that the prophet was able to do so was because the Lord had told him, *"I have put* **My words** *in your mouth"* (Jer. 1:9), and also the prophet had *eyes that were enlightened* (Eph. 1:18). He understood the visions that God gave him; he saw in the Spirit. The Word and the Spirit function together.

No eye has seen, no ear has heard, no mind has conceived what God has prepared for those who love Him – **but God has revealed it to us by His Spirit** (1 Corinthians 2:9-10).

Our response to the Lord, is to continually keep our 'suitcase' packed with His Word, so that when He comes to us by His Spirit, and asks the question, "Are you ready?" we are able to reply, "Yes Lord, I'm packed and ready to go."

CHAPTER FORTY-FIVE

BENEDICTION

May the grace of the Lord Jesus Christ, and the love of God, and the fellowship of the Holy Spirit be with you all (2 Corinthians 13:14).

The above verse is regularly used to bring a church service to a close; commonly known as 'the benediction.' It is declared as an encouragement and blessing to people as they leave.

However, there is a danger that we can become so familiar with something, that we do not appreciate its significance. That one sentence of Scripture encapsulates the message of the whole of God's Word. Everything that we discover by revelation and study radiates from the truths contained in 2 Corinthians 13:14.

It is a blessing to hear the above words as we depart from one another; but they are also a great encouragement to **begin the day**, by declaring and meditating upon them; asking the Holy Spirit to further enrich our understanding. Their truth is what surrounds us, and has been implanted into every Christian.

He called us by His own glory and goodness. Through these He has given us His very great and precious promises, so that through them ***you may participate in the divine nature*** (2 Peter 1:3-4).

It is incredible to realise that when we are born again we enter into union with the Father, Son and Holy Spirit, both for now and into eternity. The Lord wants us to *know the certainty of the truth* (Luke 1:4) that – *Never will I leave you; never will I forsake you* (Heb. 13:5).

The Father...has blessed us in the Heavenly realms with every spiritual blessing in Christ (Ephesians 1:3).

THE LOVE OF GOD

We know and rely on the love God has for us. **God is love.** *Whoever lives in love lives in God, and God in him* (1 John 4:16).

Notice the words that John used – *We know and rely on the love God has for us.* He had come to *know* God's love, and *knew with certainty* (Luke 1:4; John 17:8) that he could *rely* on His love. He had complete **assurance** – *Give thanks to the Lord, for He is good;* ***His love endures forever*** (1 Chronicles 16:34).

God does not only have love, *He is love* (1 John 4:8). God's divine nature is revealed in that one statement. Everything about Him flows from that truth. In the same manner, God does not have life, *He is life* (1 John 1:2); God does not have light, *He is light* (1 John 1:5).

Because of His great love for us*, God, who is rich in mercy, made us alive with Christ even when we were dead in transgressions – it is by grace you have been saved* (Ephesians 2:4-5).

God's love is unconditional. There is nothing that we can do to 'earn' it, either before or after we are born again – **God demonstrates His own love for us** *in this: while we were still sinners, Christ died for us* (Rom. 5:8). He did not wait until we 'got ourselves right.'

The reason that there are numerous verses of Scripture concerning God's love is that He wants us to *know with certainty of its truth* (Luke 1:4). Being *convinced* of His love towards us, which is unconditional and eternal, stops us from having a works mentality. We change our mind-set, so that we are no longer trying to gain His favour; but instead we live in the **assurance** of God's love that we have already received, and which remains.

Benediction

THE GRACE OF THE LORD JESUS CHRIST

The Law was given through Moses; **grace and truth came through Jesus Christ** (John 1:17).

The Law was given so that we would be able to recognise sin – *I would not have known what sin was except through the Law* (Rom. 7:7). It was to show that man was incapable of making himself righteous; he needed a Saviour who is righteousness itself, and by whom we are able to approach the Father – **The Law was put in charge to lead us to Christ** (Gal. 3:24).

In the Old Testament, grace was experienced – *He gives grace to the humble* (Prov. 3:34). But in the New Testament, under the new covenant, grace came in the Person of Jesus.

We have seen His glory, the glory of the One and Only, who came from the Father, **full of grace and truth** (John 1:14).

Old Testament believers encountered grace upon them; but, through Christ Jesus, we enter into His grace.

Since we have been justified through faith, we have peace with God through our Lord Jesus Christ, **through whom we have gained access by faith into this grace** *in which we now stand* (Romans 5:1-2).

Notice that the above verse states *through whom we have gained access*. His grace is not something that we are trying to attain; it is something that every born-again believer enters into when they, by faith, ask the Lord Jesus to be their Saviour.

Jesus rejoiced that His disciples accepted His words – *They knew with certainty that I came from you* (Father) (John 17:8). They were *convinced* that **grace and truth came through Him**. They then lived in the fullness of that grace.

Benediction

THE FELLOWSHIP OF THE HOLY SPIRIT

*I will ask the Father, and He will give you another Counsellor to be with you for ever – **the Spirit of truth*** (John 14:16).

Every born-again believer is anointed by the Holy Spirit – *God anointed us, set His seal of ownership on us, and put His Spirit in our hearts* (2 Cor. 1:21-22). We can be baptised in the Holy Spirit (John 1:32-34; Acts 8:14-17; 10:44-48; 19:1-7) whereby the *gifts of the Spirit* (1 Cor. 12:4-11) are made manifest in our lives. It is for every believer to receive.

Through the Holy Spirit we can *prophesy, have dreams and see visions* (Joel 2:28-32). This was fulfilled on the Day of Pentecost (Acts 2:1-21). Jesus declared that believers would *speak in new tongues* (Mark 16:17), which started at Pentecost, when they were filled with the Spirit. Paul declared that he continually *spoke in tongues* (1 Cor. 14:18). It *edifies* us (1 Cor. 14:4), and enables us to receive revelation (1 Cor. 14:2 & 15).

The Holy Spirit is the One who *guides us into all truth* (John 16:13), so that we are able to *understand what God has freely given us* (1 Cor. 2:12) through His Word. He also directs us in every-day living – *Since we live by the Spirit, let us keep in step with the Spirit* (Gal. 5:25); we do so by maturing in the *fruit of the Spirit* (Gal. 5:22-23).

There is also another dimension to our relationship with Him; ***the fellowship of the Holy Spirit*** (2 Cor. 13:14). We remain respectful of Him; but equally, we know His friendship.

We can therefore live each day *knowing with certainty* (Luke 1:4), being fully *convinced* (2 Tim. 1:12), that we have *God's love*; we are in *the **grace** of the Lord Jesus Christ*, and we have the continual ***fellowship*** *of the Holy Spirit* (2 Cor. 13:14).

SUMMARY

Continuing in faith from *believing*, to *knowing*, to then becoming *convinced* is not an end – it is a beginning.

The illustration on the front cover of this book is of the steps that we take in maturing, not only in our general faith; but also in respect of the individual truths contained within the Word of God. The top step is not to be seen as the pinnacle; it is simply a platform, from which we are able to further step into whatever the Lord Jesus seeks for us (Raymonde Harries).

We can be assured that the Lord will use us from the first day that we are saved; He does not wait until we are 'fully trained.' He sent out His disciples (Luke 9:1-6; 10:1-20) after they had been with Him for a short time. They had only just begun to *believe*. Therefore, we are not to disqualify ourselves because we consider that we do not have a full understanding, *knowing the certainty* (Luke 1:4) of all the truth in God's Word.

The issue is not where we are, but in what direction are we heading; are we maturing in Him? Are we *renewing our mind*, thereby enabling the Lord to unlock the potential within us, so that He can fulfil His plans and purposes through us?

There is a growing process that we go through in each of the specific truths contained in God's Word. For example, we can be **convinced** of God's continual grace towards us; getting to **know** the leading of the Spirit; but still be in the initial **believing** stage of understanding the authority that He gives us in Him. We need to be at peace about such matters; because we are all different, with our own individual make-up, and set of circumstances. Maturing in the Lord takes time. He is full of grace, and by His Word and Spirit, we will continue to grow in Him.

I am confident of this, that He who began a good work in you ***will carry it on to completion*** (Philippians 1:6).

#0330 - 080816 - C0 - 229/152/13 - PB - DID1539671